being of the sun

written by ramón sender & alicia bay laurel
drawn & lettered by alicia with musical
notation by ramón. songs: music by ramón
& words by alicia except where otherwise noted

harper & row, publishers: new york, evanston, san francisco, london

being . of . the . sun .

harper & row, publishers, inc.
10 east 53rd street
new york, new york 10022
published simultaneously in canada by:
fitzhenry & whiteside, ltd. toronto.

this is the first edition
standard book number: 06-012523-3
library of congress catalog card number: 73-4060

god bless you all.

we dedicate this book
to our dear father Sun
source of the earth's children
may your voice sing in every
cell of our bodies and shine
ever more from our hearts.
may we be mirrors of your light.
we love you
with your own love
O our god star

being of the sun is the companion volume to living on the earth (vintage books V-56 1971)

please feel free to color in these pages. no one has to color inside the lines. that way each book is unique.

contents

about the authors

ramón sender is the son of spanish novelist & poet ramón josé sender. he is a trained composer & co-founded the san francisco tape music center in 1962, but moved to morningstar ranch after a sun vision a few years later to make music with birds, trees, & children and be of the sun. at wheeler ranch he became friends with alicia. may 16, 1972 they were wed, after which they went off in search of a sunny place to live (and are still looking) and wrote this book.

alicia bay laurel is in love. her books to date:

living on the earth (vintage books)

earth time (1972 calendar) (random house)

sylvie sunflower (all the rest from harper & row)

the family of families

happy day, cried the rainbow lady, full of light

the earth mass (poems by joe pintauro)

ramón is ☉ ♏ ☽ ♋ asc. 24° leo
alicia is ☉ ♉ ☽ ♐ asc. 24° leo (perfect opposites = perfect harmony)

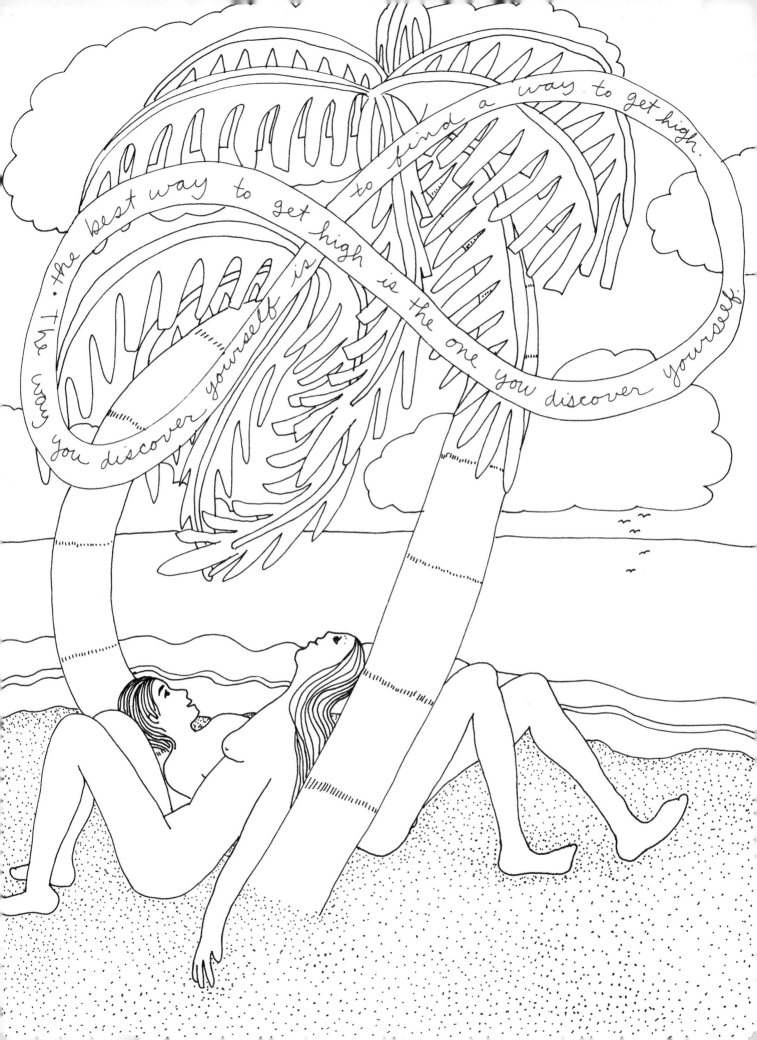

one cosmic experience of your own is worth 10,000 second-hand ones. In american indian cultures people used to have visions which became their personal religions or ways of getting high. A vision expands one's awareness and makes living easier and more enjoyable. Many beings have expanded their awareness to blissful States of at-One-ment with the universe. Some have taught other people their methods & beliefs. many have followed these divine inspirations, but one may discover one's own way, as did these teachers.

3

open yourself to the possibility of having visions.
then prepare for them by feeling your own
being and your own environment. the wisdom of
all ancient teachings lives in your heart.
when you relax enough to hear it, this wisdom
can rename you, reclothe you, give you dances,
exercises & meditations, ceremonies & recognitions
of divinity in everyday life that make your
whole day an act of being radiantly blissful.

4

there are ways of abandonment & ways of
restraint and a million ways in between,
any of which can bring you ECSTASY.

abandonment	restraint
self-expression	rules of behavior
ingestion of a sacrament	study & meditation
improvisational dancing	exercises & rituals
feasting	dietary laws
sense awareness	tuning out of senses
wilderness	temple or monastery
nudity & costumes	prescribed dress
love-making	chastity

.5

your friends can teach you ways to make
your life happier and induce bliss states.
they can teach you by example;
you need not express to the
person that they are
your teacher, nor
need you limit
yourself to one. If
you spend a night
in the same house
your souls will merge
as you sleep. If you
meet some... one who is
admirable to you in every
way, including life style, you might
surrender to him or her that they
may teach you their way. the qualities
you admire in them cannot be recognized
unless they are resonating in you at the
same time. the teacher is a reminder of
your highest self, and in that sense, your
guru is you. animals & trees are also great
teachers. mountains, wind, ocean and sun
are teachers. lessons abound for the observant.

6

every religion was born in one time & place.
they do not travel well through time & space.
at their best, each religion applies to one
person, to a family or to a tribe.

to cling to the past is to
cherish abstractions.
drawing from experience
of the here & now
is the way to find
your own religion.

the rest of this book
is an example of a
homegrown personal religion, which we
have been discovering in the here & now
of our lives and from teachings which
have inspired us. these beliefs and methods
of getting high have been discovered in
the here & now of the lives of people we
have met, so we do not claim them as ours
alone. a consciousness is manifesting
on the planet in many people at the same
time. sun yoga is as old as the sun.

7

the earth was made from
one of the Sun's ribs.
the earth is all of our mother and
the Sun is all of our father
all life comes from the divine
interaction of sun & earth.
spirit & matter
can never be separated.
we are the children
of their eternal passion.

as sun-spirits we
come into human form
until we prove harmless
to the planet. then
we can graduate to
being something
closer to the earth,
such as an animal
or a tree.

11

the sun is our model of a loving consciousness.
enlightenment is a sunny disposition.
the more you relax, the more loving
your consciousness becomes, until it shines
through all acquired conditioning and
you are as radiant as the sun.

gazing at sunlight is relaxing & quieting
to the mind. living in nature, away from
civilization, in a sunny place is the
simple road to bliss. (see warning on page 200)

life is lived with ease & grace when the self rises above the mental chatter to its true abode. a great rush of sensory awareness occurs as you enter the here & now and you discover its many 🕊 🌸 levels: the here & now of the cells of your body, of everything within you

view & hearing, of your continent, hemisphere, the whole earth (& inside her), the whole solar system. you become telepathic with these beings. the here & now of the sun is 7½ minutes in our future (the time it takes sunlight to reach the earth). living thus in the future, your movements might synchronize with the wind or the flight of birds. cause & effect merge. all is energy.

the union with solar consciousness allows you to
live in the community of the stars, who are, after
all, just you ☆ ✦in your infinite colors,
forms, ✦disguises, nebulae: the endless
playground✦ of the nameless One. your body,
transformed into light-energy and needing neither
air nor food,✦ can travel anywhere in the
solar system.

a light body has been described in
many religious writings. we like to call
it a rainbow body because its aura contains
all the colors of the spectrum.
14 the earth has a rainbow body as her atmosphere.

O SUN

creator & source of all
terrestrial life ... we developed eyes
to witness your bounteous light.
fish leap out of water into you
and crawled out onto the land
to follow your gaze. so does
the lizard love to bathe in your
light, you are his mobility.
earth life greets you rising in the east
and calls after you as you disappear;
roosters crow & cows moo with
the coming & going of your great light.
birds fly to the tree tops to sing
their evening songs in your last rays.
they follow you as our mother tilts north & south.
bees always look at you & fly toward you.
sunflowers, morning glories, all green leaves
turn to you as the Source.
the whole planet yearns to be One
with you through her creatures.
let a new golden age begin for all
of your children and
reign forever!

15

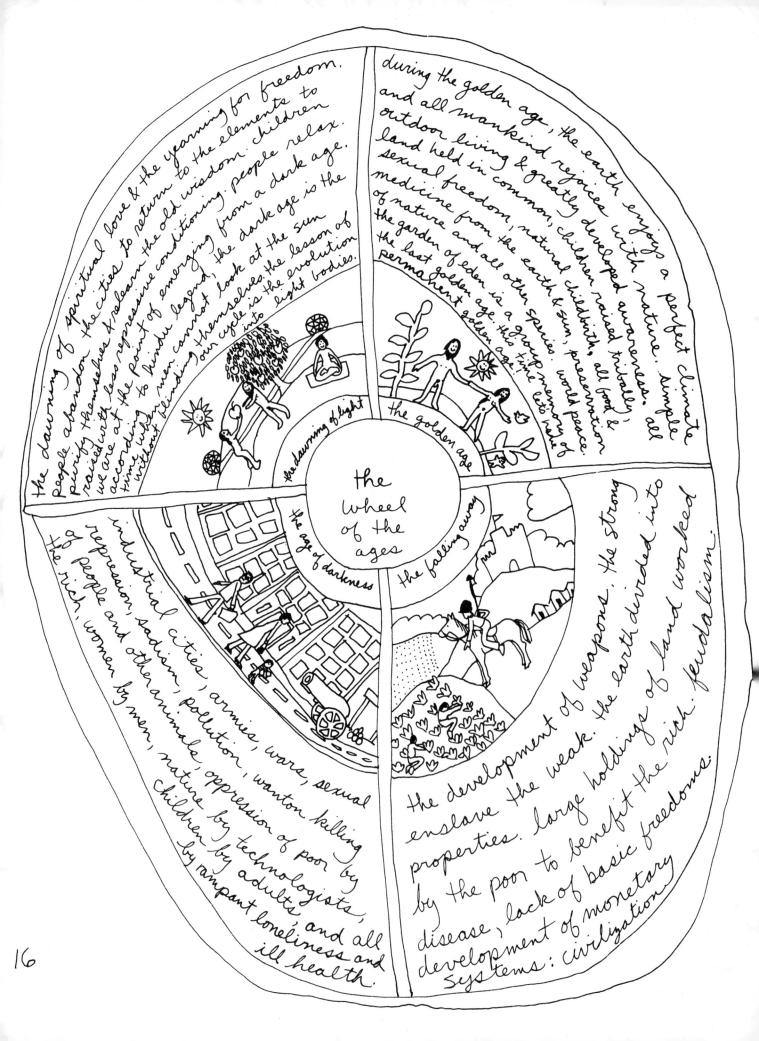

the wheel of the ages

the dawning of light

the golden age

the age of darkness

the falling away

Upper left quadrant (the dawning of light):

the dawning of spiritual love & the yearning for freedom. people abandon the cities to return to the elements to purify themselves & relearn the old wisdom. children raised with less repressive conditioning. people relax. we are at the point of emerging from a dark age. according to hindu legend, the dark age is the time when men cannot look at the sun without blinding themselves. the lesson of our cycle is the evolution into light bodies.

Upper right quadrant (the golden age):

during the golden age, the earth enjoys a perfect climate and all mankind rejoices with nature. simple outdoor living & greatly developed awareness. all land held in common, children raised tribally, sexual freedom, natural childbirth, all food & medicine from the earth & sun, preservation of nature and all other species. world peace. the garden of eden is a group memory of the last golden age. this time we have a permanent golden age.

Lower right quadrant (the falling away):

the development of weapons. the strong enslave the weak. the earth divided into properties. large holdings of land worked by the poor to benefit the rich. disease, lack of basic freedoms. development of monetary systems: civilization. feudalism.

Lower left quadrant (the age of darkness):

industrial cities, armies, wars, sexual repression, sadism, pollution, wanton killing of people and other animals, oppression of poor by the rich, women by men, nature by technologists, children by adults, and all by rampant loneliness and ill health.

16

soul mates

the sun is a great arranger of marriages
because all love emanates from its light. when you feel
the sun as your lover, the sun sends you its love manifested
in the person of your true love, in whose being the images of all beings
you have ever loved exist harmoniously. as you share more & more deeply
your here & now, you become telepathic and closer to solar consciousness.
you become the divine interplay of the sun and the earth.

17

The Four Liberating
(a yoga is a path to union with the universe)

earth yoga: generosity. making free land, food & health services available to all. ecological land use. raising all your own food & medicine. planting trees. raising earthworms. returning organic garbage & shit to the soil instead of polluting rivers and oceans. reverent use (not littering) and opening to all—the holy places of the earth (beaches, lakes, mountain tops, hot springs, volcanic craters, etc.) picking up litter. building your home & living to blend with nature & not impose upon her. protecting wild life. protecting forests. perfecting your health.
examples of earth yogis: the diggers, open land communes, ecology action groups, the hog farm. sierra club.

water yoga: love, flowing with life, speaking & acting honestly, making love, crying, laughing, hugging, kissing, touching, feeling, sensitivity to the needs of others, kindness, gentleness, sensuality, sense awareness, extended families & other new relationships, caring for the sick & unhappy. water yogis: esalen groups, communal families.

18

Elemental yogas

air yoga: truth.

telepathic communication. psychic readings. astral travel. non-repressive schools for children. student-run universities. freedom of speech in all media: truthful news reporting, underground publishers, open radio, TV, theatre, galleries. freedom of expression instead of commercial ventures. information of all government activity open to all. information of earth resources open to all. promoting world peace. tuition-free trade schools. unifying the whole earth as one people with equal freedoms & no leaders. air yogis: the world game, free universities, free schools, whole earth catalogue, non-commercial media

fire yoga: consciousness.
expanding awareness. relaxing. rising above the thought process. meditation. mantra. tuning in to the sun. finding the divine within. prayer. sacred ceremonies: making of holy times & places & things. all who are dedicated to getting high are fire yogis.

"if I am asked whether it is my nature to revere the Sun, I say again: it is! for the Sun, too, is a manifestation of the highest, and is indeed the mightiest that we children of earth are privileged to look upon.

I worship in it the light & the creative power of God, through which alone we move and have our being, and all plants & animals with us."

goethe's conversations with eckermann

everything is better out in the sunshine. meditating upon sunlight is the simplest way to get high; very pleasant sensations fill your solar plexus. The mind is cured of thought and the body of sickness. lucidity & awareness & comprehension are increased by sunlight, so learning is easier outdoors. making love in the sunshine is the greatest freedom. balance exposure to direct sunlight with variations of shade; overdosage of certain rays can damage your skin, your eyes or your hair. we won't take responsibility for anyone neglecting their bodies & blinding themselves. go slowly, gently & gradually change.

(see warning on page 200)

sunrise & sunset gazing

the sun's rays coming through the earth's rainbow aura make the colored light that plays upon the clouds, haze & even the earth herself. the band of color that the light is shining through determines what color they reflect. the pink tones are easiest to see in the blue, white & grey of the sky, but with relaxed observation, all colors can be seen.

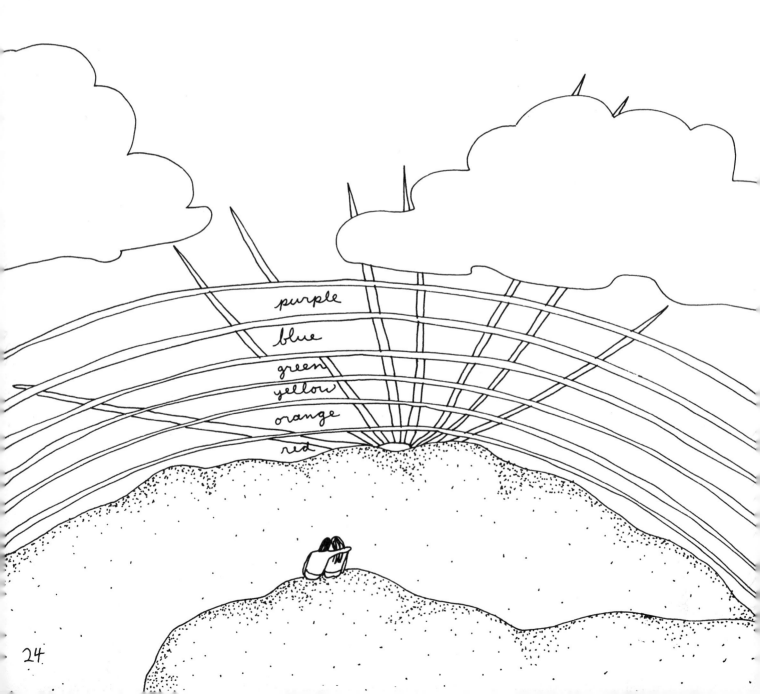

purple
blue
green
yellow
orange
red

rainbows & other wonders

when the sun is near the horizon, shining through falling rain, on the opposite horizon appears a refraction, a rainbow. sometimes when you are flying in a clear space between clouds, the upper cloud will refract the sunlight on the lower cloud as a circular rainbow with your shadow in the center. when the sun is just behind a thunderhead, sometimes it colors the surrounding vapors into auras iridescent as oil floating on water. Patient observation is rewarded with lightning, shooting stars, and all the celebrations of nature.

blue pink yellow green

red
orange
yellow
green
blue
purple

earth meditation. a mountain valley is a temple for contemplating the earth. a greenhouse makes a wonderful rainy-day meditation room. the plants can be part of your ceremony and will flourish from your attention & good vibrations.

sky meditation. a hilltop is a sky temple. tranquil contemplation can be found in the colors of the sky & the movements of clouds, as you lie on your back or do hatha yoga.

water meditations

the motion of reflected images on water remind us of the impermanence of things. to gaze upon them is soothing; to float on water is to be rocked by the great mother. bathing & swimming cleanse the mind as well as the skin, weightlessness affects the whole being. the reflections of sunlight on water make a shimmering light beautiful to look upon. the water casts lines of moving light upon cliffs, trees & walls around it. dappled shadows of overhanging leaves make dancing shapes with the movement of water. waterfalls make rainbows in sunlight. moving water produces an endless variety of drone sounds. ocean surf makes a fantastic light show, especially when viewed from above, from a cliff or a boat.

redwood, coconut palm, quaking aspen, silver
birch, each tree has its own way of filtering
sunlight. each leaf & branch performs a
different dance with the wind; each tree has
a unique voice that sings with the mother's
breath (as do we). each grove is a choir that
raises its voice in harmony when moved
by God. temples must have evolved from
sacred groves.   when a tree
died, it was   replaced by a
pillar.   temples are
groves in   countries
losing their   topsoil, like
greece and   egypt. (we
like to feed   our topsoil
and groove   in groves.)
if too many people visit a sacred grove, it soon
becomes a temple because the trees get cut down
for souvenirs and directional signs.

orchards are temples to the earth's bounty and the sun's light. by eating the fruit and burying your shit deep in the ground (leave no tracks), you plant the seeds of groves to come. even a single tree can be a sacred sun temple. lying under trees & looking up at the sunlight coming through the leaves is one of our favorite sun meditations. a book of blank pages is good to take along for an afternoon

under a tree. the sunlight makes patterns you can trace. a hammock makes a comfortable place to sit; a tire hung by a rope makes a sunstrobing seat (see sunstrobes).

just be sure your tree is strong enough not to be bent or broken by your weight.

29

our wedding ceremony took place in a temple
made of a tall pine tree and a little
30 oak that grew in a passionate embrace

plant a sacred grove

choose trees that are your favorites (ours are redwood & bay laurel). plant trees whose shade you like or whose fruit you like or whose smell you like. find out what kind of soil, compost, drainage, amount of water, and climate are most enjoyed by the species of tree and arrange your chosen site in accordance. study how the sun moves across the land. plant the trees in a circle or some other holy shape. some early sun symbols:

sumerian   astrological   wheel (evolved to christian cross)   wheel   india (the movement of the sun)

spanish cave paintings   hawaiian cross of rono (the sun god)

leave room between trees to allow for maturity. dig a hole deep enough for the ball of roots & the compost below it. (you may take a sacramental shit under each tree). give the young tree plenty of water. you may have to fence them off until they are large enough to withstand the company of grazing animals. plant flowers around the grove.

31

sing to your trees at least once a week. encourage birds to live in your grove. strive to be like the trees. play music near them. they're nice to have as friends.

to be perfectly enlightened is to be like a tree: firmly rooted in the earth, constantly adoring the sun, drawing energy from sunlight, improving the air (consciousness) around it, improving the soil both before & after death, passive to death, singing when moved to do so by the wind passing through its body.

how to join a grove of trees: hang out with them a lot. learn their language. hug them, lie next to one with the soles of your feet on the trunk. you will feel

the wind in the branches. When you are
living in harmony with their ways, they
will accept you as a junior member of
the grove & initiate you as a novice tree.

33

laurel

there was once a
nymph named daphne
who loved the sun so much
that she became totally beautiful to the sun. but in a
human body she could not give
herself totally, so she changed
into a being that lives on sunlight, a laurel tree. The leaves
of the laurel were burned on
braziers at delphi so that the
sibyls could inhale the smoke
and enter the deep trance in
which they foretold the future.
The laurel is medicine, like
sunlight; as a tea against colds
or placed over the steaming
rocks in a sauna bath.
a crown of the leaves keeps
head lice away, rolling in
a forest floor of bay
will rid a dog
of fleas.

34

redwood.
great dark quiet red-
wood trees grow in circles.
the parent tree starts young
trees around it; by the time it
dies there is a circle of tall
trees. such was the sun temple
where I first began meditating
on sunlight coming through
the branches, while lying on the
fragrant needle floor, breathing
the abundant oxygen. I talked
with them. they are among the
largest & long-lived trees; they
are patient & talk very
slowly. It's good to live
around long-lived
creatures when
learning to slow
down

35

sun strobes are devices for alternating direct sunlight with darkness, a light & shade pulse to be viewed through closed eyelids. the strobing produces colored mandalas playing on the inside of the eyelids which sometimes flash messages to you &, when very intense, produce a blissful white light state.

the simplest sunstrobe is your hands. spread the fingers of one hand and wave between your closed eyes & the sun. an opaque pin wheel works if the blades are long enough to shadow both eyes. an old black umbrella with every other panel cut out, twirled between you & the sun, works well. the world is full of strobes: windmills, electric fans, roof ventilators, running by a slat fence with the sun behind it, or riding down a tree-lined street.

sunstrobes
you can build

this is a 2-person model, one strober, one viewer.
cut out a circular cardboard disc about 12 inches
in diameter. cut out two slots, each 1/8 of the circumference
or the distance between the outer corners of your eyes.
mount it on the tip of a wooden dowel or a straight
branch several inches long with a pushpin or a
nail so that it turns on the shaft of the nail. glue
buttons near center to give a place to push
with your fingers as you twirl it over the viewer's
closed eyes as they face up toward the full sunlight.

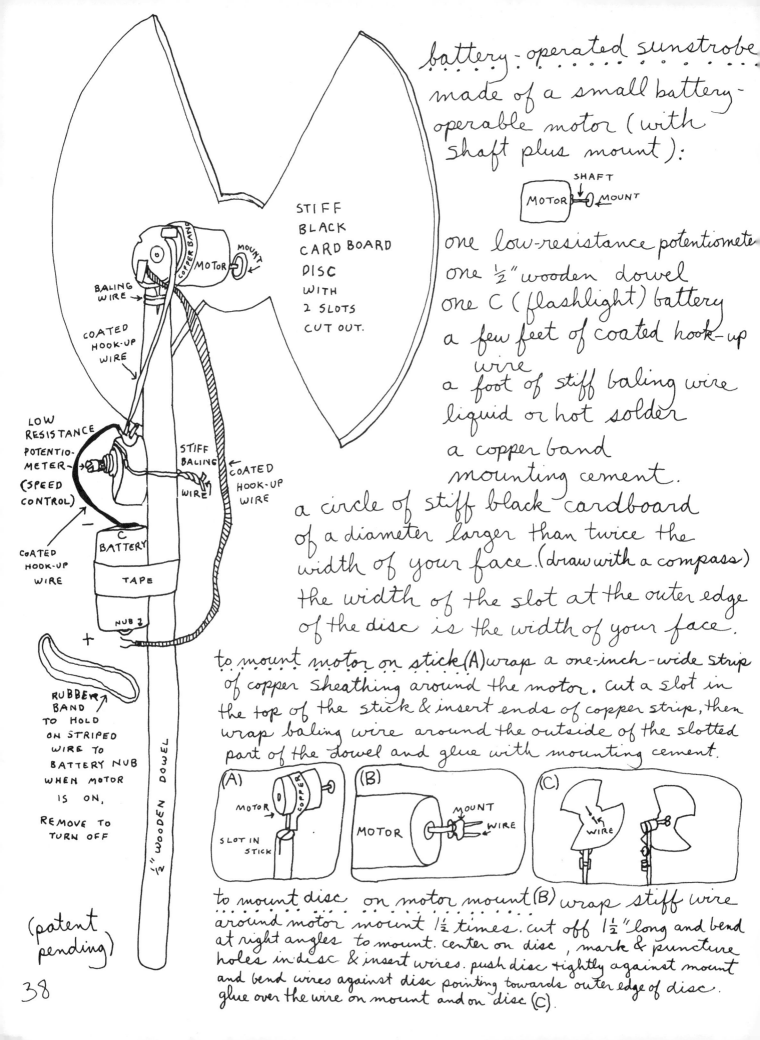

battery-operated sunstrobe
made of a small battery-operable motor (with shaft plus mount):

MOTOR →SHAFT→ MOUNT

one low-resistance potentiometer
one ½" wooden dowel
one C (flashlight) battery
a few feet of coated hook-up wire
a foot of stiff baling wire
liquid or hot solder
a copper band
mounting cement.

a circle of stiff black cardboard of a diameter larger than twice the width of your face. (draw with a compass) the width of the slot at the outer edge of the disc is the width of your face.

to mount motor on stick.(A) wrap a one-inch-wide strip of copper sheathing around the motor. cut a slot in the top of the stick & insert ends of copper strip, then wrap baling wire around the outside of the slotted part of the dowel and glue with mounting cement.

(A) MOTOR COPPER / SLOT IN STICK
(B) MOTOR MOUNT WIRE
(C) WIRE

to mount disc on motor mount (B) wrap stiff wire around motor mount 1½ times. cut off 1½" long and bend at right angles to mount. center on disc, mark & puncture holes in disc & insert wires. push disc tightly against mount and bend wires against disc pointing towards outer edge of disc. glue over the wire on mount and on disc (C).

STIFF BLACK CARDBOARD DISC WITH 2 SLOTS CUT OUT.

COPPER BAND
MOTOR
MOUNT
BALING WIRE
COATED HOOK-UP WIRE
LOW RESISTANCE POTENTIO-METER (SPEED CONTROL)
STIFF BALING WIRE
COATED HOOK-UP WIRE
COATED HOOK-UP WIRE
C BATTERY
TAPE
NUB
RUBBER BAND TO HOLD ON STRIPED WIRE TO BATTERY NUB WHEN MOTOR IS ON, REMOVE TO TURN OFF
½" WOODEN DOWEL

(patent pending)

38

wire the potentiometer to the dowel with baling wire and mount the
battery to the dowel with heavy tape or light wire.

wire with hook-up wire one motor terminal to the center
terminal of the potentiometer. attach another wire to the other motor
terminal long enough to reach the positive + nub on the battery. wire either
of the outside potentiometer terminals to the negative — end of the battery
using tape to attach wire to battery. use hot or cold solder to attach wires
to motor terminals & potentiometer. To turn it on, attach motor wire
to positive + nub of battery with a rubber band.

for indoor use, glue a centering spiral to the center
of the disc so that when the motor turns, the spiral
appears to disappear inward. this makes an
effective mandala for meditation and is sometimes
used for inducing hypnotic states.

solar-powered sunstrobe

instead of a battery, mount with
glue on the end of the motor a photo-
sensitive cell. (there are special small
motors & super low resistance potentiometers
made to run off of them.) the difference
in hook-up wiring: wire one of the wires
of the photo-sensitive cell to the motor terminal
and the other wire to one of the potentiometer terminals.
wire the other motor terminal to the potentiometer
and solder ends in place. sun turns it on. (D)

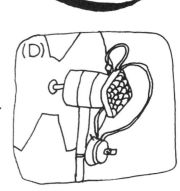

other motors

in secondhand stores you can sometimes find
battery-operated appliances that will turn the
black slotted disc ; shoe buffers, car vacuum cleaners,
desk-top fans could be wired to be sunstrobes.

39

wind-powered sunstrobes

pinwheel: cut out a square
8½" by 8½" of heavy black paper
and cut from each of the
corners to ¾" away from the
exact center of the square.

glue a card-
board circle
1½" in diameter
over the center
of the square.
make a hole with a nail through
the exact center of the square &
the circle. make holes in every
other corner of the sails (above)
when the glue is dry on the center
wheel, thread all the holes onto
a 2-inch flathead nail and pass
the nail through the center. make a
washer of a ½" of thin plastic tube or a
top of a ballpoint pen. nail to a
big thick wooden stick or a broomstick
windmills: in the shadow of
the blades of windmills you can
lie & observe the strobing, but
sometimes it's hard to get together
the directions of sun & wind.

our dream suntemple sunstrobe. a circular
structure with the ability to strobe from the
center out any amount of the roof, which can
tilt towards the ecliptic (the sun's path).
the strobe would have speed control and the roof
would be movable to control the amount of
sunlight that could enter the room. The floor
would be comfortably padded so people could
lie on their backs with their eyes closed and
meditate on the brightly colored mandalas
inside their eyelids. any inventor-architect
with a feasible design, please let us know!

how to use a sunstrobe (see warning on page 200)
lie on your back, or sit with your head back, eyes
closed and centered up in the forehead. keep
the strobing on both eyelids. keep the strobe
close enough to eyelids to block peripheral light
but don't bump your face with the disc! (for
children's use the vanes could be made of cloth so
that they flop over when the motor isn't
turning.) try different tensions of
muscles (squeezing & relaxing.)

eye

41

solar light shows

rainbow makers (refractors)

hang in a sunny place some big crystals from a chandelier. or place a fish bowl or aquarium full of water in a sunny window. wet eyelashes make rainbows. four sheets of clear plexiglas assembled into a standing triangular prism filled with water (glue with epoxy):

reflectors

mirror light sculpture: place a mirror where it reflects the sun onto an opposing wall. place another mirror where the sun hits the opposing wall, bouncing the light onto still another wall. place another mirror on this reflection and keep adding mirrors onto reflections. then light a stick of incense and dance in the middle of all the bouncing light.

mobile: make a mobile with pieces of mylar (mirror plastic) and pieces of colored plastic gels (and maybe a prism or two).

water: place a mirror at the bottom of a pan of water on a window ledge to reflect moving lines on the ceiling.

mirror balls: silver christmas tree balls reflect the sun 360°. a large ceremonial ball could be made by having an old bowling ball chrome-plated. a turning ball mosaicked with tiny mirrors sends galaxies across the walls.

filters. stained glass windows, bottles filled with water (each with a different color of food coloring in it), tent of translucent patchwork (parachute rip-stop nylon scraps: first glue together, when dry, sew together). ping pong ball, cut into hemispheres - place one over each open eye (for meditating on sunlight).

camera oscura. make a room totally dark except for a hole a few inches in diameter facing the rising or setting sun. this hole will project onto the opposite wall whatever is outside the hole in the wall, upside down. If you reflect the image onto the floor with a mirror, the image will be right side up when your back is to the hole in the wall:

mirror
hole
image on wall
image on floor
image

solar attenuators. (light volume control) latticed arbor, trees, hair, eyelashes, window shades, clouds, houses, hats: straw hats break up the sun into tiny points of light. a cloth bag of white, blue or purple cloth is good for meditating on sunlight (over your whole head). old-fashioned sunbonnets make pleasant shade.

43

a sun temple

is an environmental sculpture
given to the interplay of light & shadow.
it might include a sunstrobe ceiling
like the one described a few pages back,
plus warm baths, each with a different
color glass skylight (blue for serenity,
green for healing, violet for ecstasy). also
latticed passageways, stained glass windows,
solar & wind-operated musical instruments,
mirror balls, prisms, a greenhouse, a sundial,
domes, and the solar light   shows
on the last pages would   enhance
it.   and, of course, the   proximity
of a   sacred   grove   to complete it.

anything that exists can be perceived as a source of vibrations. Sound (existing in time) and color vibrate shapes (existing in space) in spherical from their sources.

the dropping your own the universe. Sound vibrations are called tones. the tone A is 440 vibrations per second. Benignity & malice are perceptible as "good vibes" & "bad vibes." To feel these vibrations in populous places is more

waves made by leaves onto a still pond are like vibrations going out into

difficult than in quiet places with fewer sources.

white noise

just as white light is all colors occurring simultaneously, so white noise is all pitches of sound occurring simultaneously. The wind speaks in white noise; ocean surf, the voices of trees, meadows and fire speak in white noise. the earth rumbles deeply in white noise. the colors of white noise are the vowels oh, ay, ee, oh, ooo, eye, eh. Vowel-tinted white noise is a good way to speak to earth, water, air & fire. our name for the sun is IAOUEH; the earth is OH-AH; the wind, A-OH. (whisper). water speaks in many voices, dripping, trickling, babbling, bubbling, gurgling, falling, lapping, splashing, crashing, boiling, cracking, tinkling. pouring, swirling, roaring,

his master's voice

or: how to listen to the Sun.
tune a radio between
stations and listen to the
static. during solar storms
it is much more intense than
otherwise. you can hallucinate
sounds in it, compose music from it.

at night the static is freer of other sources such
as nearby electrical appliances or automobile engines.

drones
· · · · · · · ·

a drone is a repeated tone or tones, or white noise. drones may be used to back up melodies, especially repetitive mantras or music played in modes (more about modes later). engines drone on tones, the harmonics of which you can hear as they approach & recede. when riding in cars, chant with the drone of the engine. everyone can sing a different song at the same time with a drone because they are all in the same key. instruments may be tuned to play drone backgrounds for chanting or you may tune your voice to the natural drones of crickets, flowing water, your footsteps or the wind. groups of voices and instruments can make improvisational music around a drone, taking turns droning and making melodies. birds like to be tuned to and will sing along. your breathing & heartbeat are drones. listen for drones in your environment.

harmonics

(also known as overtones. any guitarist can play some for you.)

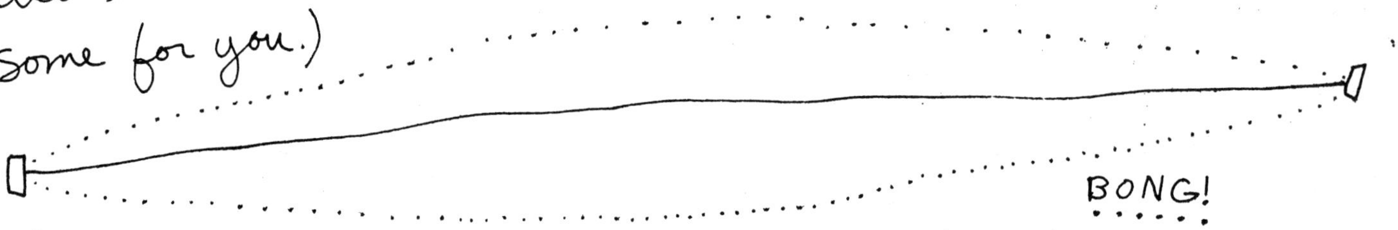

BONG!

this is a string vibrating as a whole. It makes a sound when plucked or bowed which is its tone. (middle C for example.) If you lightly touch the string exactly ½ way from one end to the other and then pluck or bow it, the tone will be an octave higher (vibrating twice as fast). this is the first overtone of the string, which, in this example, would be C above middle C. Here is the first seven of the overtone series on this string:

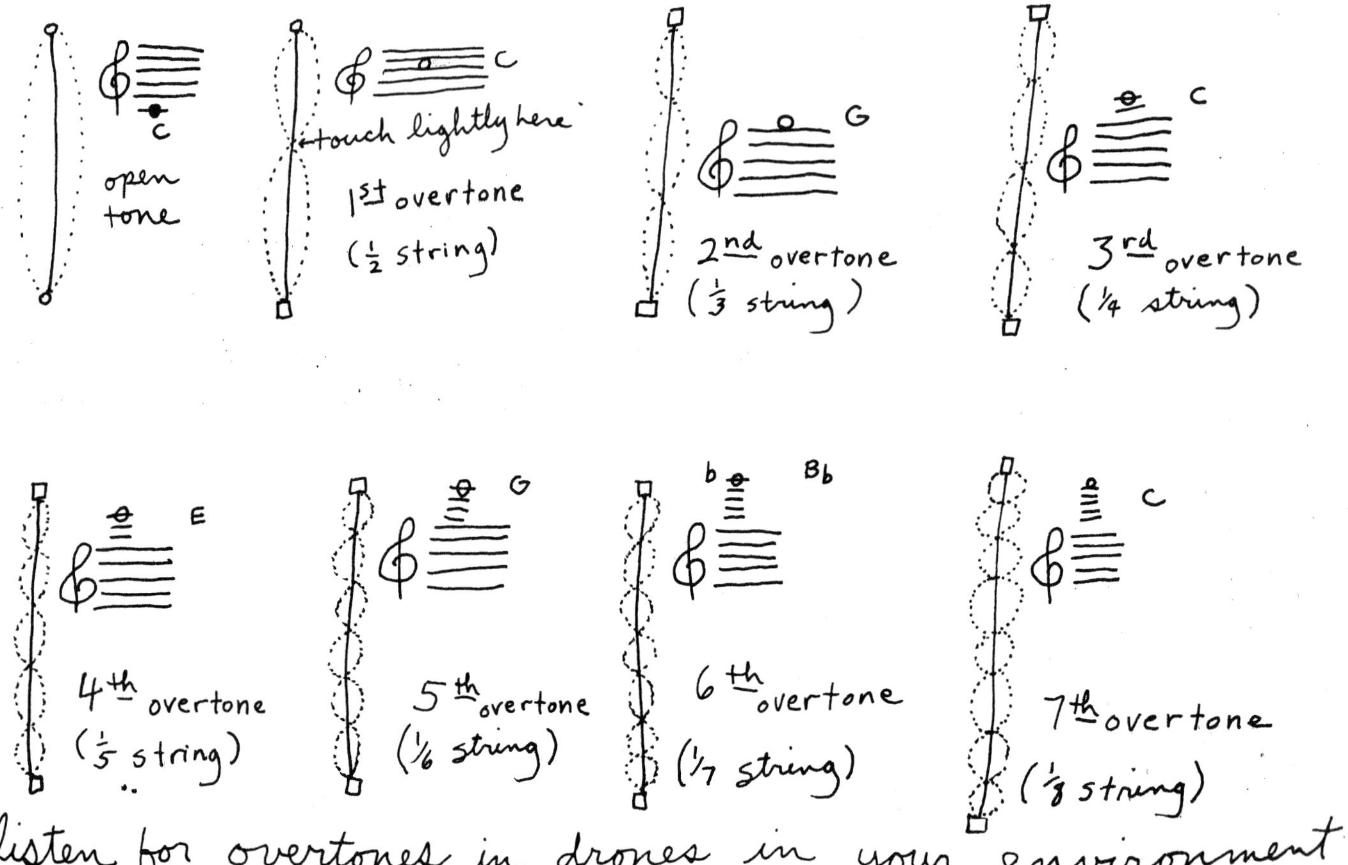

C

open tone

C

touch lightly here

1st overtone
(½ string)

G

2nd overtone
(⅓ string)

C

3rd overtone
(¼ string)

E

4th overtone
(⅕ string)

G

5th overtone
(⅙ string)

b♭ B♭

6th overtone
(⅐ string)

C

7th overtone
(⅛ string)

listen for overtones in drones in your environment (wind in chickenwire, engines, cicadas, bees buzzing).

as you go up the overtone series the interval between the tones decreases, so that the 14th overtone is approximately a quarter of a tone above the 13th overtone.

When you play a tone, all of the overtones are sounding simultaneously, though you have to listen intently to hear them. a low piano string has hundreds of overtones.

hum one tone. draw your lips into a little O and gradually open your lips as far as they'll go (as if saying WAHHH). be sure to let your palate resonate. You can make the individual overtones sound above the basic tone you are humming (especially the 4th, 5th & 6th harmonics).

the solar system as a vibrating string:

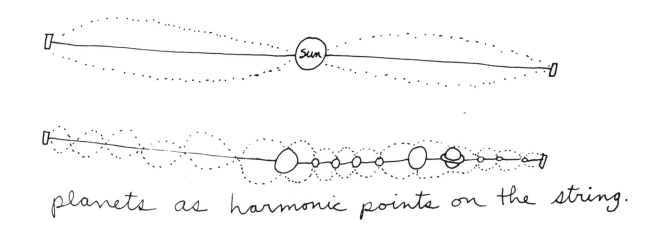

planets as harmonic points on the string.

the spine as a vibrating string:

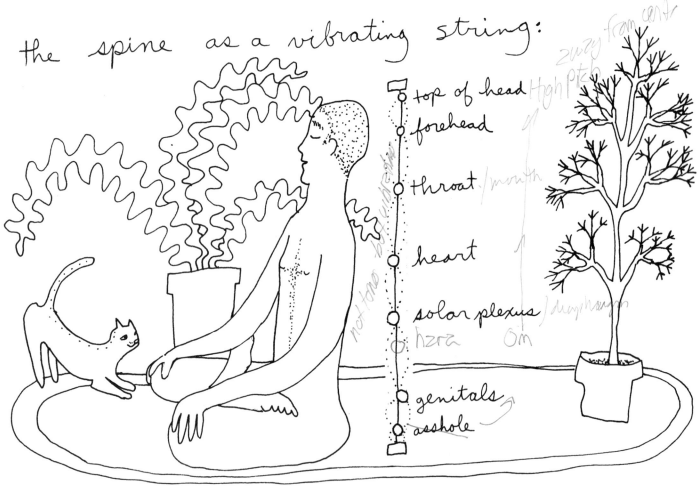

top of head
forehead
throat/mouth
heart
solar plexus
hzra   Om
genitals
asshole

the nerve centers (chakras) are like the
overtone series. If you meditate upon them
52 you can learn their individual tones and hum
their tones to stimulate them to health.

tuning by beats

when you are tuning strings to the same note, listen to the sound they make in combination. two strings that are a whole tone apart, for example C and D, make a pulsation of loud to soft (wah wah wah), with many beats (pulsations) per second:

loud

soft

(this line is one second long)

if the tones are just a fraction out of tune:

loud

soft

if the tones are in unison:

loud

soft   (there is no pulsation at all)

Ramón's mouth moves slightly as he tunes, perhaps resonating at the correct tone to aid hearing whether the string is sharp or flat (too high or too low). a guitar pitchpipe or a piano can help you find the tones. be careful not to tune strings too high or they will break. if a string won't push down more than half way, tune down to the appropriate tone to keep moderate tension.

53

autoharps
° ° ° ° ° ° ° ° °

for drone tunings, an autoharp with the machine removed has no equal, but it takes patience to tune the 36 strings. you'll need a zither tuning hammer to turn the pegs. the wire gauges vary from harp to harp, so select similar gauge strings to tune in unisons. if a string can be pushed against the soundboard, it will take a tuning up. if it can be pushed a little it is at optimum tension. If it won't push at all, tune down. If you're tuning up & the pitch isn't changing much, STOP: you're at maximum tension & should tune down. old strings especially get fragile & break easily. autoharp (or zither or santur) can be played with your fingers, with wooden mallets, with flat or finger picks, with a stick (gently stroke with the tip), a feather; good playing sticks may be found in a grove on the ground. also they can be played by babies, kids, anybody (after they are tuned properly) and are practically indestructible. Have four, pass out 3 to whoever will play, and keep tuning one, circulating it & tuning again whichever is getting out of tune (temperature affects the strings a lot). the sound is celestial.

54 open tuning for autoharp on the next page:

(open D)

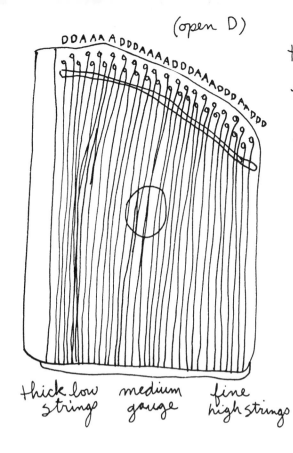

thick low   medium   fine
strings   gauge   high strings

this tuning will go with any of the chants in this book. for variation, add some E's and some B's.. or try adding to these four tones some C's & some G's but these additions will limit the number of modes you can play with. you can tune in all the notes of a mode in order of their melodic complexity (1st, 5th, 7th, 4th, 2nd notes of modal scale-more about this farther on). the more pitches you add, the more you should pluck melodies instead of stroking out drones.

guitar, dulcimer & violin

these shouldn't be tuned more than a tone above or a tone and a half below their concert tunings:

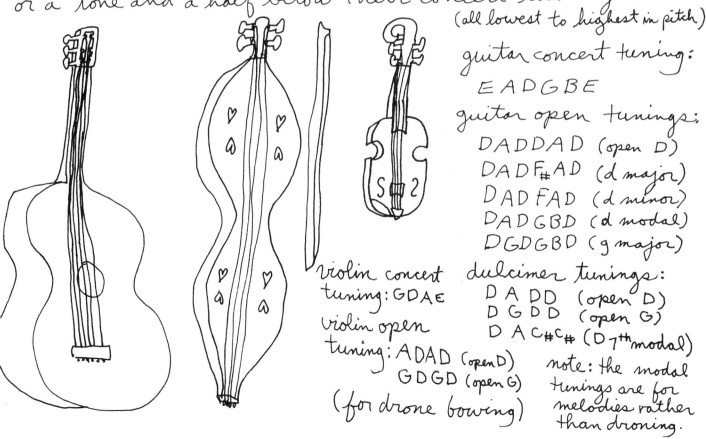

(all lowest to highest in pitch)
guitar concert tuning:
    E A D G B E
guitar open tunings:
    D A D D A D (open D)
    D A D F#A D (d major)
    D A D F A D (d minor)
    D A D G B D (d modal)
    D G D G B D (g major)

violin concert
tuning: G D A E
violin open
tuning: A D A D (open D)
        G D G D (open G)
(for drone bowing)

dulcimer tunings:
    D A D D (open D)
    D G D D (open G)
    D A C# C# (D 7th modal)

note: the modal tunings are for melodies rather than droning.

the insides of old pianos can be used like an
autoharp. several people can play it at the same
time. lay it on its side on a table. also if you
wedge down the sustaining pedal on a piano,
the strings will reverberate with sounds around it.

drone orchestra

wind chimes of varying sizes

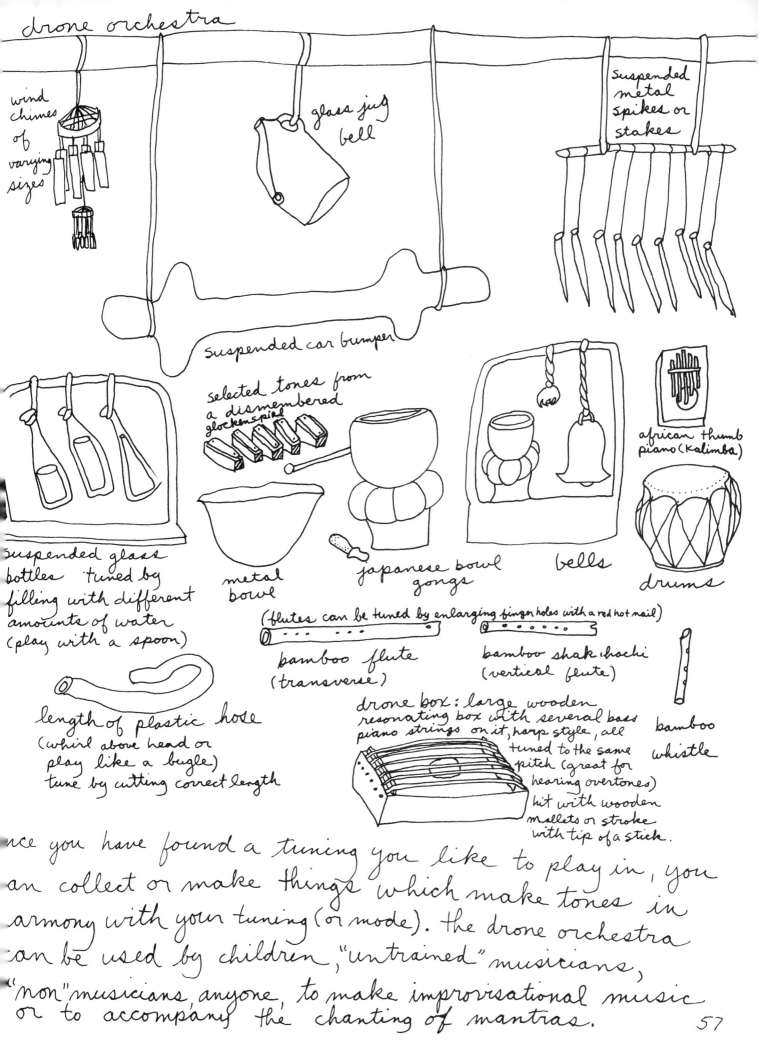

glass jug bell

suspended metal spikes or stakes

suspended car bumper

selected tones from a dismembered glockenspiel

metal bowl

japanese bowl gongs

bells

african thumb piano (kalimba)

drums

suspended glass bottles   tuned by filling with different amounts of water (play with a spoon)

(flutes can be tuned by enlarging finger holes with a red hot nail)

bamboo flute (transverse)

bamboo shak·hachi (vertical flute)

bamboo whistle

length of plastic hose (whirl above head or play like a bugle) tune by cutting correct length

drone box: large wooden resonating box with several bass piano strings on it, harp style, all tuned to the same pitch (great for hearing overtones) hit with wooden mallets or stroke with tip of a stick.

nce you have found a tuning you like to play in, you an collect or make things which make tones in armony with your tuning (or mode). the drone orchestra an be used by children, "untrained" musicians, "non" musicians, anyone, to make improvisational music or to accompany the chanting of mantras.

57

"homers" or dance whistles

junk a broken-down accordion by removing the whole set of sharp & flat reeds (the black keyboard notes). the reeds are set in pairs, one reed for the inbreath and one for the outbreath, in metal rectangles of varying sizes. cut bamboo tubes the same length and the same width of the metal rectangles. mount the rectangles inside whichever bamboo tube fits each one best. block with masking tape or pieces of wood the upper half of one end and the lower half of the other end so that air must pass through the reeds whether you inhale or exhale through it. tie a string around each one so that they may be worn around the neck. pass out all the homers to a group of people. you can dance holding one in your mouth. guitar & autoharp can play behind them, droning on the same notes (C# D# F# G# A#). If you want to make another set of homers, use the reeds of the white notes CDFGA. and still a third set from the E's & B's. color key your sets with ribbon or tape so you don't mix them up, and don't pass more than one set out at a time! large accordions have many different sets of reeds & can supply many sets of homers which can also be used in drone orchestras.

oat straw flutes

in california, the wild oats that grow by the road-side, when mature & dry, provide a tube about this circumference o (similar to a drinking straw). cut a notch below the closed end of a segment with a sharp razor:

gently coax up the reed you have cut until it rides like this:

(you can place a thread at the end of the notch to keep it open.)

if you make a whole bouquet of flutes, you'll have over half of them playable. place the flute inside your mouth all the way to the end of the notch. trying to keep the reed dry, blow as if blowing out a candle. if no air & sound comes out, try coaxing the reed to ride higher. blow again. if air starts through the reed and it clicks shut, it is not strong enough. it takes patience. tune it higher by shortening the tube. burn finger holes in them with a red hot nail (held with a pair of pliers). with practice you can play two or more at a time, a drone reed out of each side of the mouth and a chanter (melody player with finger holes) in the center. also these flutes may be used as reeds for a homemade bagpipe or a bamboo root oboe. a wide tube of bamboo makes a quiver for sets of flutes.

homemade bagpipes

close the open end of a plastic bag with masking tape. tape a piece of cardboard or leather to the end of a plastic tube to make a one-way valve (hinges open when you blow through the tube but can't open the other way.) insert tube into a hole in one corner of the plastic bag, valve end first. seal with masking tape. choose 3 oat straw flutes of similar size & strength - trim to tune them to the same tone (or one drone may be a fifth higher than the other). make 3 holes in the other 3 corners and tape in 3 bamboo tubes that will hold the oat reeds in place (the oat reeds are replaceable). insert reeds into bamboo holders, notched end first. one reed has finger holes to make melodies. hold bag under one arm with the drone reeds (in back), the tube in your mouth and chanter in your hands. blow into the air reservoir and squeeze it gently with your arm. the reeds should all respond equally to a push of the bellows. wonderful exercise for the lungs, but somewhat difficult to play.

bamboo root oboe

hollow out a bamboo root (well dried) by burning through the sections with a red-hot metal rod. then burn finger holes along one side. use your fingers to find the places for the holes. to make the oat straw reed fit snugly into the hole at the top, thicken the reed stem with masking tape to an appropriate diameter. you'll have to try many reeds to find one that interacts well with the oboe. the interaction can be described mathematically, but trial and error will provide a good combination.

yagé ceremonial flute
(from the sibondoy tribe of colombia)

thread   fingerholes   thread airhole

use bamboo 6½ inches long & ⅜ inch in diameter, a hollow tube. burn air hole ¾ inch from one end. make a wooden plug to fit inside that end. shave a little off one side of the plug and plug in with shaved side under the air hole. carve away underside of bamboo & plug to form mouthpiece. burn finger holes, one 1¾ inches from end and one 2¾ inches from end. bind with thread to keep the bamboo from splitting.

61

wind chimes

automobile junk yards are full
of sweetly resonating pieces of metal.
hang them by a string and tap with
another piece of metal to test them.
some favorites: long thick nails or spikes,
bicycle gear plates, ¼" to 1" sections
of aluminum pipe, heavy metal
circles, telephone bells (from inside
old phones), large pieces of glass
from broken windows (make deep-
voiced chimes).

the metal top from a coffee can,
punctured with nails, can hold all the hanging
things (knot a string at one end, pass through hole in
coffee can top and tie to metal object or epoxy to glass
with a piece of paper or leather over the string & let dry 24 hours).
pass four strong cords (knotted at one end) through
the bottom of the coffee can top and tie around a beam.
glue or tie strings to the bottom of each object and glue
to the end of each string a paper sail to catch the wind.

wind-driven drones. make a windmill with brushes or
wooden beads on strings at the ends of the sails that
play an open-tuned autoharp as they pass over the strings.
place bottles or tubes of bamboo in sand at appropriate
angles to be played by the wind. tune by filling with water.
tune strings on drone box together at loose tension. place
a wooden board parallel to the sound box a few inches
from strings and place so wind goes between strings & board.

water drones: listen for the tone of a waterfall of a a small cascade. carefully move the rocks at the base of the other waterfalls until their tones are the first & second overtones of the deepest sounding waterfall. vessels of metal, glass or wood can be placed under falling water (off a roof) to make melodies with water. earth drones. a whole pasture full of cows with harmoniously related bells around their necks.

chanting. when not absorbed in the sounds of nature
you can join the birds, water & trees in lifting
your voice in praise of your maker. The difference
between a chant & a song is that a chant is
repeated many times and can be accompanied
with drone music. (also see "mantras.")

if you're chanting indoors, sing up & down the
scale, listening to the sound. on a certain tone the
room will "boom" — you will have found its
resonance. On that tone chanting & droning will
have the full deep echo of the room singing along.

for outdoor chanting we have evolved a set of
modes & keys to sing & play in which we feel
are harmonious with the hours of the day and
the phases of the moon. first we choose the key
by the phase the moon is in. let's say it's a full
moon and the time is 6 AM. the drone would be in C
and the mode would be mode 7, which is a major
scale with a sharp 4th and a flatted 7th. sing the scale
& play on your instrument a few times to learn it. then
you can improvise a song from it or use the scale (by
numbers) to change the melodies of the chants in this book.
if the scales are too hard, chant on the tone of the moon, or speak it.

music chart for ceremonies & chanting
· · ·° ° · · · · · · · · · · · · · · · · · ·
(with colors for environment)

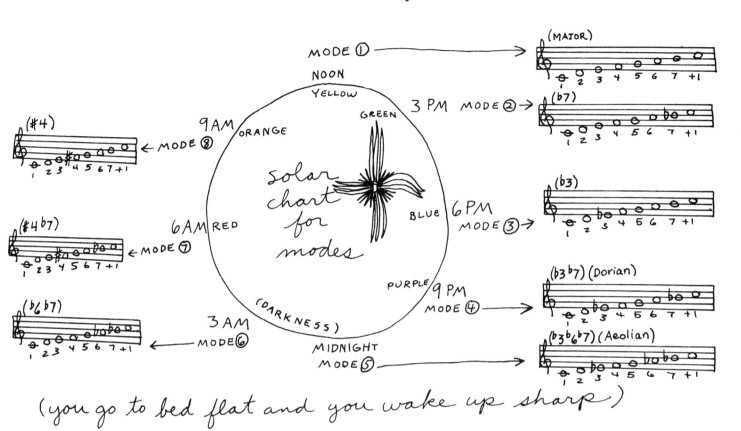

MODE ① ——————→ (MAJOR)

NOON
YELLOW
GREEN

9AM ORANGE   3 PM MODE ② → (♭7)

(#4)
← MODE ⑧

6AM RED   solar chart for modes   BLUE 6PM MODE ③ → (♭3)

(#4♭7)
← MODE ⑦

PURPLE 9PM MODE ④ ——→ (♭3♭7) (Dorian)

(♭6♭7)   3 AM   (DARKNESS)
MODE⑥

MIDNIGHT MODE ⑤ ——————→ (♭3♭6♭7) (Aeolian)

(you go to bed flat and you wake up sharp)

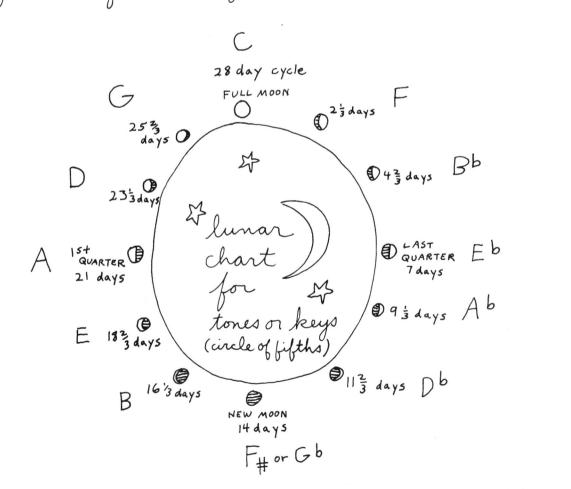

C
28 day cycle
FULL MOON

G   F
25 2/3 days   2 1/3 days

D   B♭
23 1/3 days   4 2/3 days

A   1st QUARTER 21 days   lunar chart for tones or keys (circle of fifths)   LAST QUARTER 7 days   E♭

9 1/3 days   A♭

E   18 2/3 days   11 2/3 days   D♭

B   16 1/3 days

NEW MOON 14 days

F♯ or G♭

cloudy day modes. these are more difficult &
more exotic and complex:

the chants in this book have numbers below the notes. if you
read them by the numbers, you can substitute any of these modes
for the ones the chants are written in.

twelve hands across the sky

67

how to tell time by the sun

with your hands: stand with one arm outstretched toward the place where the sun came up. make the thumb side of your hand appear to rest on the horizon and the little finger side parallel to the horizon (palm away from your face). each distance across your hand above the horizon is one hour. there are 12 hands across the sky during the equinoxes, from 6 A.M. to 6 P.M.

9 AM

sundial: find a round stump cut flat or canted to the south. Set a stick straight up in the center & mark hours by observation (12 noon the shadow points due north). as the seasons change, the shadows change, so you'll have to mark new ones. After a year it will be complete.

NOON

observatory: in the center of a large flat meadow, preferably a hilltop, place a stone to sit on as the fixed observation point. (you may place a sundial to read from this point as well). mark the solstice & equinox sunrises and sunsets with large stones or logs at the edges of the field (these places are also the rising & setting points of the band of zodiac stars at night). the observatory can be used as a ceremonial grounds for solstice, equinox & eclipse celebrations and for full moon meditations (see holy days chapter)

equinox sunrise

69

a whole day with the sun

4AM to 6AM (violet-red)

when you awaken, observe your sleep breathing (its pace, where the sounds come from in your body, what parts you move as you breathe) so that you can copy it thoughout your day. chant the AUM to remember your dreams. observe the perfect stillness of nature, the return of colors the return of your lover's face. the moon in its last quarter and the morningstar rise before dawn. good time for meditation.

6AM to 8AM (picture next page) (orange)

all of nature greets the sun; songs of birds fill the air; roosters crow; sunflowers turn their heads; dew begins to rise. take your morning shit & analyze your health. Bathe or swim or just splash your face and back with cold water. do hatha yoga or other stretching dances. make bed, open windows, arrange house & altars. sing morning songs. time for milking & feeding of animals. breakfast with fruit and herbal tea. gather herbs when in full flower.

8AM to 10AM and 10AM to noon (yellow)

the morning work hours: gardening, playing with children, building, making beautiful things, dancing, hiking, walking meditation. survival work or thankless tasks done without thought of reward. observing nature.

seven work-hour ceremonies:

spend the time alone, silent, listening, not thinking

spend the time silently with someone you love
    (develop telepathy)

feel all muscles, bones, nerves, organs, skin moving in a relaxed way.

make an anonymous gift or good deed.

whistle with the birds; learn their language.

feel the sun as lover, friend, brother, father.

rise above your thoughts & observe your self.

when gathering food, be sure to thank the plant or animal who is giving of itself, give your care in return. make your creative work a gift to the universe.

noon to 2 P.M. (yellow-green)

noon meal: nuts, seeds, sprouts, fruits, greens, dried fruits, goat cheese, fruit or vegetable juices, yogurt or whatever suits you best (those are our favorites). after cleaning up eating place & vessels, hang a hammock in a piece of perfect shade and take a nap. observe all the other animals at this hour, especially dogs, cats, cows, goats, horses, lizards, snakes, butterflies, birds, fish and bees. listen to the air, watch the clouds or the flow of water. relax all over. listen to drones in your environment and tune to them. sing the noon chant.

MODE ①
TONE ©

Noon Chant

Hey! there you are on high   the bright-test ho-ur of the day

win-king thru the trees and clouds   gol-den on the mea-dow.

2 PM to 4 PM (green)

afternoon work hours are like the morning work hours, though you may have changed projects. in the planting of flowers, washing of clothes, fixing of broken things, or whatever you are doing, feel how the sunlight is helping you. if you are not working, lie in a grove and watch the sunlight come through the leaves or make music with children.

TO THE SUNLIGHT

We are lear-ning to use your po--wer to ease our sur-vi-val as you ri--pen our pa-pa--yas and cul-ture our milk, raise our bread dry our figs warm our house and wa-ter dry our clothes melt the snow dry the mud and our a-do--be bring the herbs to flo-wer heal our wounds, ste-ri-lize our jars lift the fog from our gar-dens and il--lu--sion from our minds.

4 PM to 6 PM (blue)

the winding up of the day's work & the preparation of the evening meal. water the garden; milk and feed the animals; put away your tools and toys. listen to the sounds of water as it flows to the sea. Salads, soups, tea on the table, hold hands in a circle around the table and chant the AUM or the solar grace:

feed the first bite to someone else. on receiving this bite, chew it 100 times. we like to eat cloves of raw garlic with our evening salad to encourage health in the digestive tract. take your time & enjoy every bite. Clean up eating place and vessels. listen to the evening songs of the birds in the treetops.

6 PM to 8 PM (indigo)

watch the sunset & chant the sunset chant:

at sunset:
Mode ④
tone ©

can be sung at noon:
mode ①
tone Eb

Sunset Chant   RS'67

On-ly thou, oh ri-ver of de--light   on-ly thou thru

end-less day and night   on-ly thou   as--sua-ger of all

repeat 101 times or repeat until the sun disappears.

Sor---row   on-ly thou, oh gi--ver of to-mor-row

For Mode ④ sing as follows: 5 ♭7 +1 ♭7 5555 5, 5♭7 +1 ♭7 etc.

aum & chant to drones tuned to the crickets. listen to the night songs. meditate on the evening star, the waning of the light, the revealing of the constellations; the rising of the full moon.

Prayer for Night

tone ©
mode ⑥

we face a-way from our ma-ker   in-to endless space and star-ry

fa-mi-lies   in the light of the moon our sis--ter

our ma-ker is re-flec-ted   to bless our eyes in her tran-

-quil-li-ty   the dark-ness of our mo-ther earth en-folds our peace.

night time (violet - black)
meditate on the stars being your brothers and
sisters (be the sun). hug someone & feel the
sun shining inside their body. When making
love, first remain
joined together
without moving
for as long as
you can, looking
into each other's
eyes & synchronizing
your breathing.
as you go to sleep,
try to remain
conscious of
what happens
to your body.
the hours before
midnight give
the most refresh-
ing sleep.

84

The Last Song of the Night

ABL '70

D modal

Voice / Guitar

It's the last song of the night it's the last song of the night

we're go-ing to lie down but
we're go-ing to our beds but
we're go-ing to -- sleep but

we'll still hear the sound of the last
e - choed in our heads is the last
in our hearts we'll keep the - last

song of the night

each day is an opportunity
to truly help mankind
in your potential
to relaxation & bliss.
your peaceful vibrations
affect everything & everyone
around you.

the lunar cycle

the full moon. a time so full of high energies and gatherings of water in the environment & in the body that it is often difficult to sleep. an all-night meditation may be occasioned by the full moon. we have discovered some points on which to focus which are harmonious with the signs of the moon; one is given in each monthly celebration. the highest tides of the month occur in the full moon.

the 3rd quarter. gradual decrease in energy, a good time for unwinding from busy days & nights

the new moon the lowest tides of the moon's cycle, a time of serene emptiness and silence.

the 1st quarter. the regathering of energies. time to start projects and do most intense work. hope is renewed and excitement grows.

3rd quarter
NEW MOON
FULL MOON
1st quarter

chants for the phases of the moon

tone © mode ② Full Moon Rising

O-range at sun-set blue at mid-night yel-low in the dawn when a ring sur-rounds you your light is milk from the hea-ven-ly blue ud-der to-night the tides have ri-sen full and we are floa-ting a-bove our heads.

tone E♭ mode ④ Half Moon (3ʳᵈ Quarter)

Rise at mid-night at dawn I saw you at the top of my sky Some of the cric-kets were still sing-ing un-til the day be-gan and you both dis-ap-peared.

New Moon

tone F♯ mode ⑧

I can-not see you un-less you shade the sun But I feel Si-lent and in un-i-ty with the sun I know where you are.

* If too many #'s, ignore and sing in F with no B♭ and with an E♭ here.

tone Ⓐ mode ②

Half Moon (1ˢᵗ Quarter)

Once a-gain u--pon the sky co-ming o'er the top at sun--set Ligh-ting my way home un-til mid--night I will plant my gar--den in the wax-ing of the moon.

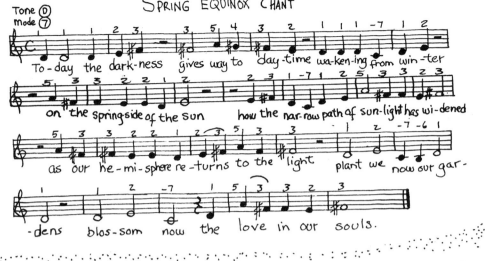

SPRING EQUINOX CHANT

Tone ⓪
mode ⑦

To-day the dark-ness gives way to day-time wa-ken-ing from win-ter
on the spring side of the sun how the nar-row path of sun-light has wi-dened
as our he-mi-sphere re-turns to the light plant we now our gar-
-dens blos-som now the love in our souls.

vernal equinox is the festival of air

the vernal equinox celebration: make windchimes, kites, wind-powered drones or a wind machine and assemble on a hilltop or a beach. sing spring equinox song & other drone music accompanied by the wind. AUM over seeds, seedling and baby animals. make egg tree & egg worlds flags & banners.

wind machine

wind catching cups nailed to poles
ribbons & cardboard decorations tied to poles
bells, windchimes tied to poles

the poles are all attached to a tube which rests on the pole in the ground and can move freely around on it

bury deeply & reinforce with rock or tie to stakes on 4 sides. it is very top heavy.

full moon in libra (full moon is always in the opposite sign of the sign the sun is in) - meditate upon the sky & the upper atmosphere.

egg tree

make a small hole with
a nail at both ends of an
egg, and blow through one hole
so the yolk & white come out the
other end into a bowl. (use in a
cake or omelet.) dry the shells
overnight. decorate them with
paint, beads, tissue paper, lace,
ribbon, paper cut-outs, etc. (white glue
works well). glue thread or ribbon to
one end (with a bit of paper over it to secure
it) and dry thoroughly. tie them to a
potted tree or a fallen branch potted
in rocks or hung from the ceiling. this
is an indoor decoration - weather can
hurt the paper.   after the holy day, wrap
the egg shells in tissue paper, store
in a box for next year's. my (A) mother
has some I made 15 years ago!

egg worlds

after blowing out & drying the
egg shell, widen one hole
enough to build a little scene
inside it. old dentists' tools,
tweezers, toothpicks can help
you glue the tiny paper cut-outs
in place. the scene faces
the smaller hole - when the
construction is complete, glue
a piece of transparent tissue
paper over the big hole to be the
sky behind the scene and look
in through the small hole, aiming
the sky at a light. my (R) sister
makes little forests & chapels
with stained glass windows!
carefully decorate the outside
of the egg, too.

91

the month of taurus ♉ april 20 - may 20

apple blossom time: go out in an orchard &
listen to the songs of the birds. select five of
their favorite tones to make a 5 tone mode.
then get 10 to 50 pieces of aluminum conduit
pipe and cut them so that they chime on your 5 tones.
drill two holes near one end of each chime and hang
in pairs from the trees so that the wind will
knock them together and make the whole blooming
orchard chime with the songs of the birds.

planting a garden after the soil is prepared
to receive seeds and young plants, decorate the
garden fence with streamers, god's eyes of
bright colored yarn lashed around sticks, a
beautiful scarecrow & other gestures of
good will to the plants. Plant fruiting & leafy
crops in the waxing of the moon and root crops
in the waning of the moon. the water signs (cancer,
scorpio & pisces) are the most fertile moonsigns.
moon in taurus is also good for root crops and moon
in libra for the planting of flowers.

full moon in scorpio: meditate upon the arctic
poles, on ice & snow & tundra, glaciers & snow-
capped mountain peaks.

planting day ceremony

CHANT

(to the plants)

CHANT

Tone Ⓒ
mode ①

(to the earth and sun)

Let the e-le-ments be har-mo-ni-us

wel-come these chil-dren of the sun and

bring them to fru-i---tion

You are col-lec-ting sun-light for us   we will bring you

wa-ter   we will bring you com-post mulch and poles to lean on

we will sing your prai-ses   and pro-tect you from blights

frost and pass-ing deer herds   will you give us your sun-

-light   when the earth col-lects your bo-dies?

93

may day

° ° ° ° ° ° ° ° ° °

dancers: sew jingle bells onto bright colored ribbons which the dancers can tie around their wrists, ankles, arms, waist or head as they choose. each dancer holds the end of a ribbon of the pole facing clockwise & counter-clockwise alternately. when the music (drone of harps and flutes) begins the clockwise-facing dancers go outside the first person they meet, inside the next, outside the next and so on. the counter-clockwise do the same only they start by going inside the first person they meet, until the pole is wrapped. the pole may be unwrapped & danced again.

may wine: add woodruff to white wine the day before (or drink mead—honey wine).

may pole: tear up bright colored rags & old clothes into strips 2 inches wide and as long as possible. divide into piles by color and tie together to make ribbons 20 feet long, each a different color of the rainbow. tie by cutting a slot one inch long, one inch from the end of the strip on both ends of all of the strips. then attach:

and pull taut.

staple all the ribbons to the top of a pole at least fifteen feet long & 3 inches in diameter. then tie each ribbon once around a barrel hoop a foot or so below where they were stapled. (you can add extra streamers or a cut-out decoration on top). dig a hole (with a post hole digger) 3 feet deep in a meadow suitable for dancing. a may pole made this way can last for years.

95

weddings: choose a good planting day & have the ceremony near a garden or orchard (the growing things give & receive blessings on these days). when everyone has assembled, the person closest to the couple imparts a blessing as they sit in two chairs. then all the men lift the bride's chair and all the women lift the groom's chair and carry them in a procession with music to the table where the cake is. the couple cuts the cake & gives a piece to each person at which time anyone may bestow good wishes upon them. then much music & dancing.

wedding cake make 3 round rich fruitcakes of three different sizes using whole wheat flour, honey, chopped nuts, chopped dried dates, figs, raisins (roll each piece in flour so they don't stick together), tahini (sesame butter), and grated orange peel, ground cinnamon, nutmeg, cardamom & a little salt. cover a tray with pieces of wax paper and place the largest cake on top. ice it with a mixture of honey, shredded coconut, and tahini well stirred. place the second largest on top of the first and ice it, then place the smallest cake on top and ice it. cut an orange through the center and place a slice on top. cut thin wedges to decorate the sides. pull out the pieces of wax paper from under the cake. decorate the tray with tiny vases of fresh flowers.

full moon in sagittarius meditate on lightning, people's auras, the flow of energy.

96

an alone wedding ceremony. find a magic place in nature and make an altar with a comfortable place to sit, musical instruments & a bowl of fruit. sit together in tantric yoga meditation, make music & feed each other slices of fruit.

love prayer.

oh endless bliss
stretching from lover's kiss
through the whispering wind
through the center of the sun
to the birth of galaxies
all paths meet in thee. RS '69

DMODAL or Regular tuning

THE SUN IS FOREVER A LOVER

The sun is for-e-ver a lo-ver
The earth is for-e-ver our mo-ther
but we are all just pas-sing
and gives us the love that she

thru
can
so don't sit and think on for-e-ver
but all we can give to each o-ther
and is the

love 'til the day breaks
love of a fel-low man
through
look in my eyes and I'll

look in your eyes
lord can't you see it shine?

don't hide be-hind all the thoughts in your mind and love 'til the day breaks

through

ABL '71

97

the month of cancer ♋ june 21 to july 22
....
summer solstice (the festival of water)
....
swimming, sunbathing, hanging of banners, hammock swings and awnings. drone music & AUMing in gardens, orchards & greenhouses. on a shady beach or hilltop make a picnic of early summer fruits and vegetables with much singing, dancing and lying around watching sunlight coming through the treetops or sunstrobing in the full sunlight. at high noon a great shout, blowing of conchs and beating of drums: hooray for the Sun! summer solstice chant:

Tone ⒟
Mode ④

5 5 5 5 7 5 5 4 5 5   5 7 5 4
You have reached the high-est in our hea-vens   and the wi-dest

3 1 3 4 4 4   5 7 5 5 4 4 4 3 5 1 -7
span of our ho--ri-zon   as we tra-verse the sum-mer side of the

-7 1   5 5 5 5 7 5 5 4 5 5
SUN   we are in the joy of your at-tend-ance

5 7 5 4   3 2 3 1 -7 1
u--pon this half of our   mo-ther's breast

full moon in capricorn : meditate upon the soil,
on gardens, orchards, forest, jungle or ocean floor.

98

cut a
rectangle of cloth
and hem the ends
over a stick of
wood. tie string to
both ends of the upper
stick (the lower one
is to weight it down).
sew patches of cloth
to the center to make
pictures or mandalas
if you use heavy
nonabsorbent fabric
like canvas, you can
paint on it. hang
them on walls or trees
on festive days. 99

awning
make a banner & lash two more
sticks to the end sticks to hold
it up. place a stone in the center
and tie string around it on the outside
and tie to a beam or branch. sew
cloth to the sides and secure to
stakes at corners using stones & string.

the month of leo ♌ . july 23 to august 22

name-changing ceremony. at a tribal gathering, a person who has recently had a vision might stand up & say "to remind me of the great nameless One and to recognize my true self, I ask you to greet me as (new name)." then a drone chant of the person's new name for several minutes will help people remember it.

anointing ceremony. to be performed by four to six friends upon one person, before he or she is to be wed, or after a heroic deed, or as a group gift. massage should follow a bath or swim. Spread towels on a floor, bed or table for the recipient to lie on. use these oils:

oil of mint: center of forehead, back of neck, temples
oil of rosemary: hair & scalp (a great conditioner and doesn't leave oiliness or smell).
wheat germ oil: whole body. rub firmly, don't pinch, knead towards the heart. almond oil is also good, especially on fingers & toes.
coconut oil (if solid, warm it up): genitals, asshole.
perfumed oil (patchouli, lemon verbena, sandalwood, rose etc.) on wrists, behind ears, neck if the person prefers it to his sweat.

full moon in aquarius. meditate on the farthest reaches of outer space—.

one oil anointing.. wheat germ oil

foot anointing... wonderful after a long hike. wash
the recipient's feet in warm water and rub
them with salt while wet. Rinse in clean warm
water and dry thoroughly, especially between
the toes. then oil the feet and ankles.

freeform ceremonial dances.
maintain a loose pelvis; you will feel pleasant
sensations rush through your body when your
spine undulates from the movement of your
pelvis. the movement of your knees is the
key. conga drums make the best dance music.
earth dance: move with great effort as if through a
medium of thick jello. water dance: move as if
swimming, floating or skin diving. air dance: move as if
flying, gliding. fire dance: radiate a great warm light
from the center of your chest. unfolding to the sun:
begin curled on the ground and slowly grow like a flower.
group dance I: make eye contact with each person you meet.
don't talk. group dance II: eyes closed, make body contact with
each person you meet. couple dances: dance with one part
of body (other than hands) always touching. take turns losing your
balance & being steadied. simultaneously explore each other's bodies. 101

prasadam is a food offering to god in all beings. it can be cornmeal on a bird feeder, dried fruit offered to friends on a hike or hours working in the kitchen of a free food mission or a large commune. It can also be placed on altars in nature: a tree stump feast for local wild animals (deer like oats, raccoons like dogfood, rabbits like raw vegetable parings), or crumbs for fish & ducks in a pond, or compost in the earth for the earthworms and green growing things.

prayers are conversations with your god-self. they can be thought, spoken or written. first you name your desires — changes you'd like to see happen in yourself, in your environment. when these are listed, count your blessings and offer thanks for these. by this time if an action on your part is necessary for the fulfillment of your wishes it should be evident. little bits of advice will pop into your head from god-knows-where. listen to all your voices and then relax and let the changes happen. if it is a written prayer, sometimes it's fun to shelve it for three months and then reread it to see if your wishes had any effect or whether you outgrew them.

full moon in pisces: meditate on clouds, fog, vapor, mist; the movement of water through air.

a visit by a very special holy person deserves a feast and lots of ethereal drone music. make a necklace of fresh fragrant blooms: with a darning needle and a long piece of button thread, string the flowers together by piercing the base of each flower so that they all face away from the thread. then several smiling people can carefully place the necklace around the holy person's neck, and sing the welcoming chant.

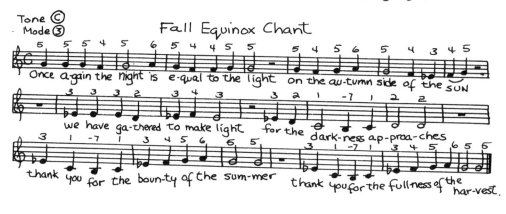

Tone Ⓒ
Mode ③
Fall Equinox Chant

Once again the night is e-qual to the light on the au-tumn side of the SUN
we have ga-thered to make light for the dark-ness ap-proa-ches
thank you for the boun-ty of the sum-mer thank you for the full-ness of the har-vest.

the autumnal equinox (festival of earth): rake up fallen leaves into piles and jump in them or lie on them. make a pit and light a fire in it. roast potatoes & unhusked corn, drink hot cider AUM around garden, orchard, cellars, grain bins and canning closets. AUM over the oven while baking sunbread. at sunset go to a hilltop to sing the fall equinox song, the sunset chant & other drone music.

full moon in aries. meditate upon fires, flames, candles, bonfires, kerosene lamps.

ceremonial sun bread

make whole wheat yeast bread dough,
knead it and let it rise to double in a
warm bowl covered with a cloth. oil a large
cast iron skillet. separate the dough into
three large parts and one small part. roll
the small part into a ball and place it in
the center of the skillet. Roll the three large
parts into ropes one to two inches thick.
braid the ropes and place the braid in the
skillet surrounding the ball. attach the ends
of the braid so that the circle is continuous.
cover with a cloth and allow to rise again;
bake at 400°F   (or whatever temperature
your bread   recipe calls for). When
almost   done, brush the
top   with a mixture
of   an egg yolk and
one   tablespoon of
water   bake 10 minutes.
        hand-sized
        chunks can
        be torn off
        as the bread
        is passed
        around a circle.

variations: roll a fruit or cheese filling inside
each rope (& the ball) before braiding.

the month of scorpio M, october 23 to november 2.

birth ceremony. AUM with the mother during contractions. Softly play tinkling drone music after the child is born; let him enter the world to the sound of angels.

death ceremony. dig a deep hole as long as the body of the dead person. place him in it naked and bury up to two feet below the level of the ground, and plant the favorite tree of the person over the grave. all this should be carried out silently. after the burial, all witnesses may abandon themselves to a wild revel of song & dance somewhere away from the grave.

moving in to a new house. make a procession going into the rooms, opening windows and burning cedar shavings or dried bay leaves in a frying pan or stone dish. AUM in a circle in each room. moving out of a house. clean and arrange it with the next occupant in mind.

full moon in taurus. meditate upon the center of the earth, on volcanoes & the creation of mountains, minerals & continents.

Onward Onward Ever Flow

the month of sagittarius ♐ november 22 to december 21

harvest festival . . . in the middle of a table
assemble a bounteous tray of the most
beautiful fruits and vegetables you have
grown or gathered. surround the tray with
paper harvest goddesses (see pages 110-111) and
invite neighbors to bring their best
culinary masterpieces to share. AUM
together holding hands around the table
and anyone can make an extemporaneous
prayer of thanks for the bounty of the earth.
after the meal more candles are lit, music
& dancing begin & the table is cleared by everyone.

full moon in gemini . . . . . meditate upon weather
systems, air currents, wind & seasonal changes

Thanksgiving Song

guitar: regular tuning

ABL oct. '69

Ear-ly spring-time flo-wers a-bound ev---ry-thing sings
sum-mer ri-ver wa-ter-falls gleam o-----cean bound
au-tumn's boun-ty co-vers the earth fra-grant with food

ba-by birds are fly-ing a-round try---ing their wings
time to take a Swim in the stream bo---dies turn brown
mo-ther na-ture's bo-so-my girth bril-liant-ly hued

So we go to plan-ting our seeds in the ground
So we go to ten-ding our gar---den so green
So we go to har-vest the fruits of the earth

Soft the Ap-ril rains come fal-ling fal-----ling down
strong the sum-mer sun is shi-ning shi---ning se-rene
warm sep-tem-ber winds come laugh-ing ca---rol-ling mirth
Oh, the year's sweet gifts un-fol-ding day --- and night

So we go to plan-ting our seeds in the ground.
So we go to ten-ding our gar---den so green.
So we go to har-vest the fruits of the earth.
So we thank our ma-ker for gi----ving us light.

back to ✳ on
3rd time thru

109

harvest goddesses to grace autumnal feasts
are easy to make. trace these shapes and
cut them out of strong white paper or colored
construction paper. color them in or collage
them with bits of magazine pictures. then glue
them to an empty toilet paper roll as follows:
first glue the blouse around the roll, lining up
the top edge of the blouse with the edge of the
roll. then glue the skirt around the roll, lining
up the hem of the skirt with the other edge of
the roll. (glue on the inside of the waist and on
the glue tab only). then glue the arms to the arm
sockets and the glue tabs of the feet to the inside
of the roll under the front of the skirt. glue the
face to the front   hair and glue this united
piece to the   inside of the roll so that it
faces the front   of the dress. then glue the
back of the   hair to the front hair, matching
the edges. then   glue the tab on the bosom to
the neck on   the inside of the roll and gently
tuck the   ends of the breasts into the
blouse &   secure them with glue.
you can   put name cards or paper
fruits or   musical instruments in the
hands. add wings for angels or a bouquet of straw flowers.

III

the month of capricorn ♑ december 22 to january 19
· ° · ° · ° · ° · ° · ° · ° · ° · ° · ° · ° · ° · ° · ° · ° · ° · ° · ° · ° ·

Winter Solstice Chant

Tone Ⓔ
mode ⑤

our half of the earth has tipped a-way from you and we are on the

win-ter side of the sun when we are in cold and dark-ness

we see you in can-dle flames and fires we have stored your en-er-gy to

feed us un-til the time you warm us thru our skin.

winter solstice. at midnight gather at a hilltop
to make a bonfire if it is still, if windy, find
a sheltered hillside or use an indoor fireplace
if the weather is inclement. make a warm
drink for all present (mulled wine, spiced tea,
hot cider, hot spiced milk). much hugging and
laughing and exchange of found or handmade
things. at midnight sing the winter solstice
chant and old favorite songs & carols. burn
candles on metal plates in windows to
guide travelers to shelter for this is the
darkest night of the year.

full moon in cancer. meditate upon the ocean
& the flow of waters over the earth: lakes, rivers
rain, inland seas, & the blood of land creatures.

Receiver - Believer

regular tuning

if you're loo-kin' thru the night for a place to take your ease a
if you're sing-in' on the paths of the gar-dens of the sun come

can-dle still shines from my win-dow if you're loo-kin' thru the world for a
sing a verse with me thru my win-dow if you're loo-kin' to the past for

gar--den of peace bet-ter stop your tra-vlin' on and look with-in no one can
glo-ry gone un-sung you've still to see the glo-ry be-gin tho' tho'

tell you a-ny-thing you don't feel in your heart you can get it straight you're no
to-day

lon-ger a-part from the all ri-ver flo-win' the all gi-ver know-in' the

all re-cei-ver be-lie-ver re-cei--ver be-lie-ver

song of my soul sing it now sing it whole sing it all in a cir-cle sing with-

out and with-in all are one be-ing sun-beam be-lie-vers

ABL '71

113

Green Green Rains

D MODAL D   C9   D   D

1. Green green green green spring val-ley fo-rest sun smi-ling shy gent-ly
2. fall fall fall thunder showers in the au-tumn dark clouds shout for their
3. long long long long cold win-ter nights rains seem to call out a
4. C9 pray pray pray for the sun to come back sun shi-ning warm on our

Emi7   D

cal-ling   back the rain from the grass turn turn sum-mer
roa-ring   po-wer songs to the grass turn turn win-ter
war-ning   of a flood and the grass cries cries in the
bo-dies   that have grown with the grass green green in the

C9   D

brown 'til the green when the mud like a winter when the

D   C9   D

ABL '69

green green rains come fal-ling
green green rains come fall-ing   5. repeat first verse
la - dy all co-vered for mour-ning
ri - ver came up to the cot-tage

keeping warm if you are in a heated room, place a pan of water over the heater to keep your nose from drying out. winter health is improved by taking sauna baths often.

eclipse of sun or moon cut a small hole in a big piece of cardboard and let the eclipsing sun project through it onto a wall (camera oscura), & watch it happen on the wall. lunar eclipse can occasion an all-night meditation. eclipse chant:

Tone © SLOWLY
Mode ⑧ 1 3 4   5 5   1 3 4 5 5 6 5 5 4   5 3 2 3   23 1 -7 1 2 1 1

Just for one mo-ment we in one line cast a sha-dow earth and sun and moon in-ter-play of light and dark-ness.

full moon in leo meditate on the sun & the light of the sun, in you, in all terrestrial life.

sauna bath.

construct a dome 5½ feet high in the center and about 10 feet in diameter, either of curved branches buried one foot in the ground & lashed together at the top or a small geodesic dome. in the center dig a pit. near the walls spread hay & over that some cloth. cover the sides of the dome with construction plastic and insulating blankets and bury all the edges in the ground so that there are no leaks. build a fire with large rocks stacked in with the burning logs. (volcanic rocks are best, igneous are better than sedimentary). after 3 or 4 hours of steady burning carefully dismantle the fire with a pitchfork and shake the hot rocks to get the cinders off, carry them into the dome & place them in the pit. fill 10 one-gallon containers with water & place in the dome for people to drink or wash themselves with or wet the rocks.

then everyone enters naked & finds a place to sit or stand (very careful of the hot rocks in the center) and the door is closed so no hot air leaks out. after the dry heat suffuses the dome, sprinkle a little water on the rocks. the steam is very hot! when the dome is cloudy with steam, place a small branch of fresh bay laurel, yerba buena or mint or eucalyptus on the rocks. People may sing or chant or massage or wash each other or meditate on the steam. one person may stand bent limp from the waist while two people stand on either side of him and drum up and down his spine with the little-finger sides of their hands until they are tired. then the person in the middle straightens up one vertebra at a time without speaking, feeling very tingling all over. (the other two should be prepared to steady him if he's dizzy). when each person has had enough heat, he leaves the dome, shutting the door tightly & takes a cold shower or a swim in a cold stream. they may re-enter the dome and repeat the process until they feel completely purified or the rocks are cold. after drying off, rub wheat germ oil on the skin. caution: don't use river bed rocks as they can explode when heated.

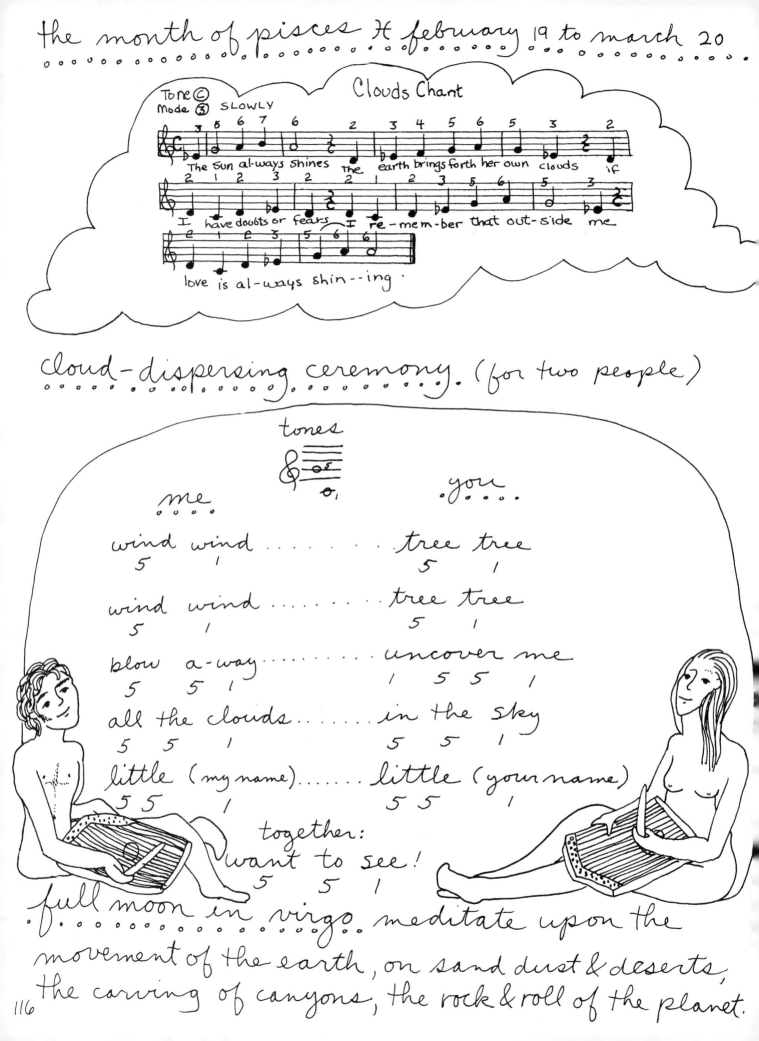

the month of pisces ♓ february 19 to march 20

Clouds Chant

Tone ©
Mode ③   SLOWLY

The Sun al-ways shines   the   earth brings forth her own   clouds   if

I have doubts or fears   I re-mem-ber that out-side me

love is al-ways shin---ing.

cloud—dispersing ceremony. (for two people)

tones

me.   you.

wind wind . . . . tree tree
5   1   5   1

wind wind . . . . tree tree
5   1   5   1

blow a-way . . . . uncover me
5   5   1   1   5   5   1

all the clouds . . . . in the sky
5   5   1   5   5   1

little (my name) . . . . . . little (your name)
5 5   1   5 5   1

together:
want to see!
5   5   1

full moon in virgo. meditate upon the
movement of the earth, on sand dust & deserts,
the carving of canyons, the rock & roll of the planet.

116

elemental dances of abandonment.

earth dance run up a grassy hill or a sand
   dune and roll all the way down.

water dance. float upon ocean surf. let
   it carry you to the shore.

air dance. run around a windy meadow
   with an umbrella. let it lead you.

fire dance run naked in the sunshine.

rainy days run naked in the rain.

regular tuning

Rain's Falling Down

C   C

rain's fal-ling down how the drops fill the air trees are
o-ceans are crash-ing the moun-tains are still and the

a minor   a minor

green
rain co-vers all   all a-round grass is thick ev-'ry-where and a
like the wind has no will but the

C   C

sigh fills the space 'tween the clouds and the ground be-tween
clouds blow in-land and the earth   a-round and a-
turns

a minor   a minor

hea-vi-er drops it's a far a-way sound fal-ling
-bove all the clouds sun & moon shi-ning down shi-ning

*D⁹   G⁷   C   *D⁹   G⁷   C

down all a-round pas-sing by thru the sky
down all a-round pas-sing by thru the sky

ABL '68

* 1ˢᵗ inversion
(F# on bottom)

117

we're all going to the same place; the difference is the time it takes.

don't mind Flow if her pace is slow;

we're all doing the best we can.

118

meditation & hatha yoga

119

mind is buddha, while the cessation of conceptual thought is the way. once you stop arousing concepts and thinking in terms of existence & nonexistence, long & short, other & self, active & passive, & suchlike, you will find that your mind is intrinsically the buddha, that the buddha is intrinsically mind, and that the mind resembles a void. only come to know the nature of your own mind in which there is no self and other, & you will be in fact a buddha.

huang-po
(9th century zen master),
translated by
john blofeld

120

the mind
· · · · · ·

to use the full capacity of one's brain is to experience simultaneously everything happening in the here & now, from the cellular activity of the body to the farthest reaches of the universe. sensory perception is mental, but it is not thinking, which is talking to oneself without making any noise. thought filters out sensory awareness. meditation is a way to rise above the thought-maker into the the realm of here & now, bliss.

breathing

to begin a meditation breathing. feel your you inhale, your expand (relax) and it should contract breathe through your your mouth, and diaphragm (belly) rather observe the rhythms

relax your asshole. When asshole should when you exhale (draw up).

nose rather than breathe from your than your chest. & sounds of

your sleep breathing as you wake up, and copy them in meditation & daily living. the sound of your breathing should come from your chest & throat rather than your mouth or nose. try out some long gentle sighs.

breath counting technique

each inhale or exhale counts one number.

you can do it a variety of ways: our favorite
is

in	out	in	out	in	out	in	out	in	out	in	out
1	2	3	4	5	6	7	8	9	10	9	8

in	out	in	out	in	out	in	out	in	out	in	out
7	6	5	4	3	2	1	0	1	2	3	4

and so forth. this concentration exercise
may be enhanced by the visualization

1 1

of the numbers, approach-
ing from a distance on
the inhale, and receding
into the distance on
the exhale. you
can do it with
eyes open or
closed.

energy currents

as you relax your breathing you begin to feel your whole body pulsating. then you become aware of currents of energy within the body. Usually it starts as a tingling sensation in the hands or feet, spreading in waves through the whole body. The flow of this energy (called prana in sanskrit) can be directed at will throughout the body. You can "breathe" it in through your nose and out through your toes or in through your toes and out through your nose. You can breathe it in through the palms of your hands and out through your heart or the center of your forehead. You can breathe in a figure 8, inhaling down your spine & curving forward into your belly, and exhaling around your crotch, up the lower spine & out through the chest. the early hours of the morning are the most tranquil & full of invigorating prana. the hours before midnight give the most refreshing sleep.

124

the eyes may fix
relaxedly on a
candle flame, a
mandala (design
flowing out from a
center), the moon,
a dried sun-
flower center,
a drop of dew,
a fragrant
blossom, a
star, the eyes
of another
who is gazing
in your eyes;
or the void.
(or see the
sunlight
meditations
in this
book).

to
contemplate
the void:
fix your
eyes on a
point in space
4 feet in front
of your face.

125

positions for meditating.
sit with your spine straight
and shoulders relaxed. rock
your body back & forth until
you find a comfortable place
to stop. you can sit cross
legged or in   a chair
or in lotus   or ½ lotus.
you can wrap   cloth
around your   knees
and the small   of your
back. tibetan   monks
make wooden
boxes to brace
the back & the
knees. zen monks
sit on firm
round pillows.
you can also
sit on your
heels.

you can meditate
while walking:
neither stiff
nor slouching,
balancing
firmly on
both feet,
each step
an exhale
or an inhale
as slowly
as you can.

you can meditate lying down, but
most people who try it fall asleep. mudras
or hand positions will help you stay awake:

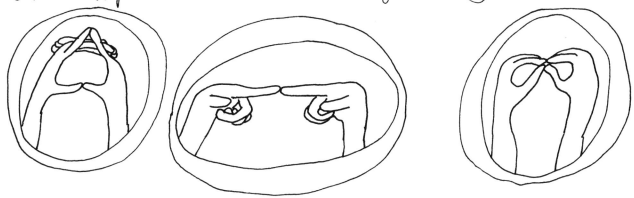

this tibetan hand mudra is traditionally
done standing on one foot with the sole of
one foot against the inside of the thigh of the
other leg, but you can also do it on your back:

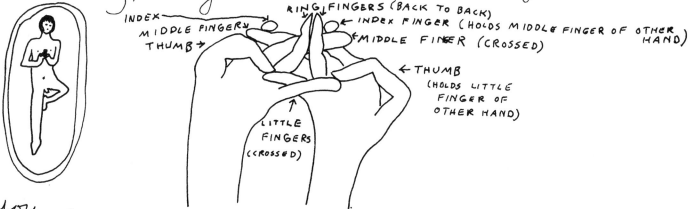

INDEX
MIDDLE FINGER
THUMB →

RING FINGERS (BACK TO BACK)
← INDEX FINGER (HOLDS MIDDLE FINGER OF OTHER HAND)
← MIDDLE FINGER (CROSSED)

← THUMB
(HOLDS LITTLE
FINGER OF
OTHER HAND)

↑
LITTLE
FINGERS
(CROSSED)

you can make up your own hand mudras.
this one is our favorite for lying on our backs in
a grove watching the light come through the leaves:

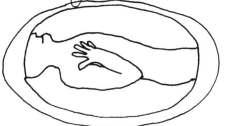

mantra

a word or words that get you high can
be repeated rhythmically: as a method
of rising above the thinker, as a meditation,
as an act of loving devotion to the one, as
a greeting, or as an accompaniment to
dancing or other mindless activity. drums,
finger cymbals, drone instruments, hand
clapping and wind chimes are good with
mantras. you can breathe them, sing them,
whisper them, speak them or chant on one tone.

speaking mantras

BOM SHANKAR BOLENAT "thank you, god, for reminding me that I am the Universe." (a good greeting)

MAY ALL BEINGS BE PEACEFUL & HAPPY FOREVER (say it 6 times - once to the earth, once to the sky and once in each of the four directions.)

breathing mantras

Shanti (peace) inhale "shan" exhale "ti"

So ham (I am He) inhale "so" exhale "ham"

singing mantras with melodies

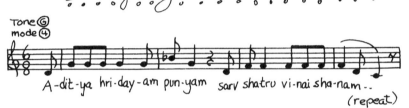

Tone ⑥ mode ④

A-dit-ya hri-day-am pun-yam   sarv shatru vi-nai sha-nam.. (repeat)

this means, in sanskrit: "all evil vanishes from him who keeps the sun in his heart".

Tone ⑥ Mode ①

Now

nuh nuh now now now nuh nuh now now now nuhnuh now now now now

nuh nuh now now nuh nuh now now now nuh nuh now now now nuh nuh

now now now now nuhnuh now now nuh now nuh now nuh

nuh nuh now now nuh nuh now now now now nuhnuh now now

repeat

.......this one goes well with fiddle, dulcimer & jaw harps

singing mantra on one note

the gayatri (at the beginning of the hatha yoga pages) is one of our favorites. begin with an AUM and then sing the rest on the same note as the AUM. when repeating it, sing an AUM between each verse.

AUM

is a name for the all in sanskrit and
is the source of the latin word omni,
meaning all, also the word amen.
it is a chant of open & closed mouth
humming on a single tone. begin singing

ah (as in f<u>a</u>ther), then O (as in b<u>oa</u>t), then hum
mmmm. each AUM takes one long exhale. you
can hear the harmonics on the tone you're
singing as you move your lips. a room filled
with hundreds of people AUMing sounds like a
tremendous bell. besides being an effective
meditation mantra, AUM is a fine way to say
grace before a meal or conclude a meeting of
130 close friends. AUM together holding hands.

an altar is a meditation environment.
here are the elements we like to include:

mandala

sunstrobing provides many designs for these circular & symmetrical shapes flowing from a center. draw them often and you will find one that really draws your gaze, which can be used as design for an embroidery, painting or prayer rug. Inward curling spirals turning on a wheel are good. (see sunstrobes)

dish of water
light reflected in water is relaxing to look at.

incense.
keeps time (five minutes or more per stick). keeps insects away. provides a point to gaze on, odor makes a tranquil mood. place a dish underneath to catch the ashes.

candles.
illuminate altar when surrounded by darkness, provide points to gaze on. candlelight, like sunlight, is easier on one's nerves than electric light.

bowl gong.
or a resonant bell or flat gong is a bringer to the here & now. the decaying sound can be centered on when beginning meditation. also good for punctuating singing and chanting or the beginning and end of a session of meditation or hatha yoga

natural things.
for their good vibes. sea shells, potted plants, dish gardens, smooth stones.

a comfortable place to sit

131

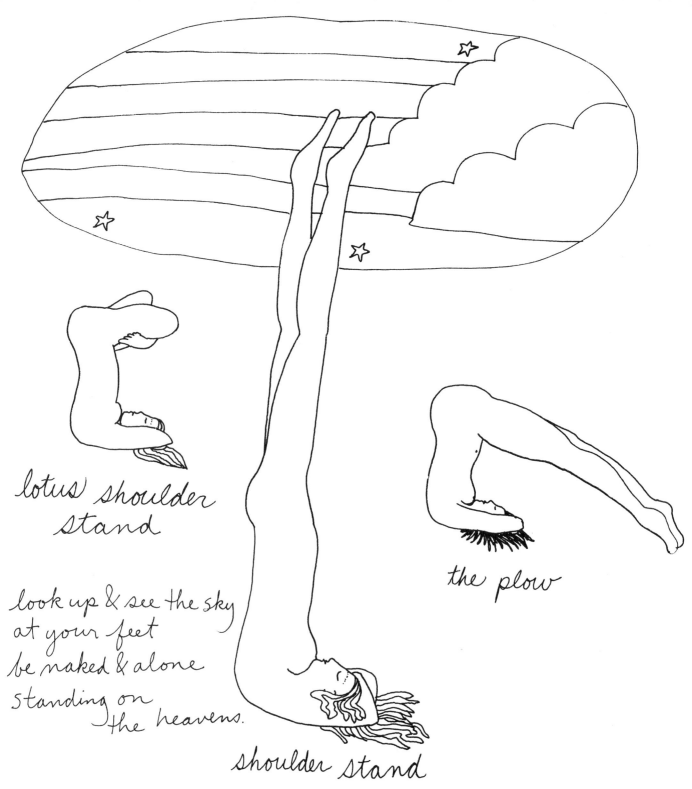

lotus shoulder
stand

look up & see the sky
at your feet
be naked & alone
standing on
the heavens.

shoulder stand

the plow

we are not teachers of hatha yoga, but we submit our
routine as an example of what can be developed for
personal use. if you try them, please do them slowly &
gently, resting between each posture. the aim is
not how many you can do, but how many relaxed breaths
you can hold each one without straining. If you feel
132 sore afterward you've been pushing too hard. Take it easy!

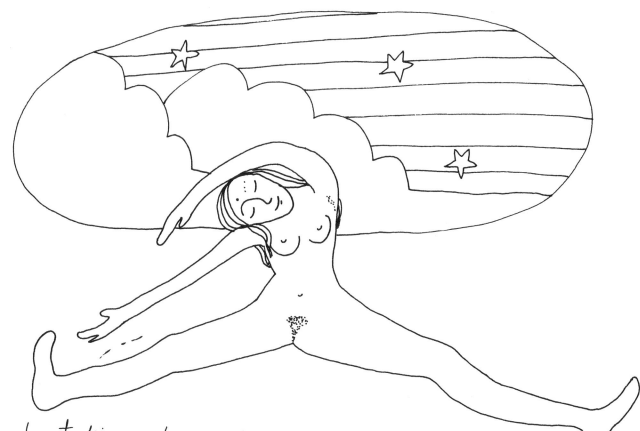

the best time to do the asanas (postures) is in
the morning before breakfast, after having
taken a shit and if possible a bath or a swim.
the best place is on a flat, clean, firmly padded
surface, such as a folded blanket — if possible
do them nude outdoors in the cool sunshine
or warm shade. a morning like this makes us
feel good all day. Hatha yoga strengthens the back,
quiets the mind, stimulates blood circulation, calms
nerves, takes off excess flabbiness & limbers up
the whole body. It enables you to sit or stand
without leaning on anything. If you have a hatha
yoga teacher watch & correct your asanas it will
save you much time & struggle. Rest between poses
as many breaths as you spent doing the last one.

our hatha yoga sequence

the gayatri mantra is one of the oldest hymns
known to man. it is chanted to the rising sun.
below is ramón's translation from the sanskrit.
sing it on one tone several times, slowly:

AUM Bhûr Bhuvah Svăr
Tat Savitur Varenyam
Bhargo Devasya Dhimahi
Dyo yo Nah Prachodayat

AUM oh earth, oh air, oh golden light
oh that sun, most adored
we drink the splendor of that God
may he fill our day with light.

eye exercises

A. alternate looking up as far
as you can and down as far
as you can for several relaxed
breaths.

B. then alternate from side to
side as far as you can for
several relaxed breaths.

C. alternate upper right to lower
left and upper left to lower right

D. roll eyes clockwise and
counter clockwise.

surya namaskar (greeting to the sun). If you have time to do
only one exercise, do this one. The 12 poses
are the months of the year.

A. face sun with palms
together in greeting.
breathe out.

B. breathe in as
you lean back
with palms over head

C. touch the floor
in front of feet
(breathe out)

D. breathe in as
you bring right leg
forward, left leg back.

E. hold breath as
you bring right leg
back.

F. breathe out. touch floor
with forearms, hands, forehead,
chest, knees and toes

G. breathe in as you rise
up with legs, hands
& stomach on the floor

H. repeat E
breathing
out

I. repeat D
breathing in
with left
leg forward

J. repeat C.
breathe out

K. repeat B.
breathe in

L. repeat A
breathe out

STANDING ASANAS

the mountain:
Stand with weight equal
on heels & balls of both feet.
contract belly and relax
shoulders with spine straight.
Observe slow breathing.

the tree:
start in the mountain
pose. lift one leg so that
sole of foot is on inner
thigh and knee goes out
to the side. Place palms
together over head with
arms straight. Observe breath.

additional: these three
poses before returning
to the tree and then the
mountain. then do the
whole pose again on the
other foot.

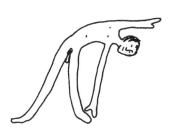

stretches: with knees
straight bend over to one side
with arm outstretched and
touch foot with other hand.
observe slow breathing.
do both sides.

ceiling stretch: rise on
tiptoes and stretch whole
body up with palms parallel
to ceiling. hold for as many
relaxed breaths as you can.

the cow: touch palms
to the floor (or ankles)
and hold as many relaxed
breaths as you can.

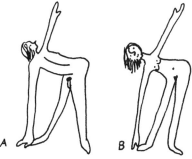

triangle toe touches:
spread legs with knees
straight. A place right hand
on left foot, extend left
arm above head & look at it.
B place left hand on left foot
and look at right hand above head.
Then both poses on right foot.

extended foot pose.
spread legs with knees
straight and feet parallel.
place palms in line with
feet between them. If easy,
place palms together with
fingers toward head behind
your back. Observe slow
breathing.

rooster pose:
stand straight with
palms together behind
back, fingers toward head,
and place one foot a step
in front of the other. A:
stretch head to knees.
B: stretch head towards buttocks.
change feet. observe breath.

135

flying: stand straight with palms together, arms straight over your head. if you do this one slowly you can get several relaxed breaths in each pose. A: stretch upwards B. lunge forward onto right foot C. stretch back flat, shift weight onto right foot. D. balance on right foot with arms extended forward and left leg extended straight back. E. stretch arms out from sides. when done perfectly the head, palms, left foot, knee, and the whole back are the same distance from the floor. F. return to standing position. do it again on left foot.

LYING PRONE & ON BACK

the locust: lie prone with arms at sides. Then lift legs, arms & head, without bending elbows or knees. hold several relaxed breaths and then lie prone again.

the bow: lie prone with arms at sides. Then lift head and grasp ankles with hands. (you can bend your knees). hold several relaxed breaths and then lie prone again.

the cobra: lie prone with palms on floor beside shoulders. look up, bend head back & lift up chest using arms as little as possible. hold several relaxed breaths and then come down head last.

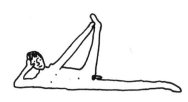

anantasana: named for the serpent upon whom the god vishnu sleeps & dreams the universe. lie on one side with lower elbow outstretched & palm on ear. stretch up the upper leg and clasp foot with upper hand. hold several breaths. then do the other side. try not to bend your knees.

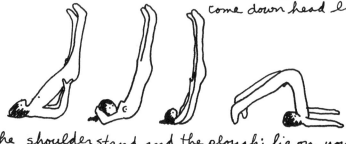

the shoulder stand and the plough: lie on your back with arms at your sides. bring your legs & back up so that all your weight is on your head and shoulders. your arms can be in either of 3 positions shown above in order of easiness. hold as many relaxed breaths as you can. Then bring feet over your head to the floor (legs straight) and stretch arms out straight on the floor behind your back. hold this pose several relaxed breaths then bring your feet straight up again and come down slowly with legs straight, one vertebra at a time. you may feel a satisfying crack or two as your vertebrae are on the floor and you slowly lower your legs (don't bend knees).

KNEELING & SITTING

get loose: stand on hands and knees. A: lift up back, lower head and bottom, breathe out. B: lift up head & bottom, lower back, breathe in. alternate these two for several relaxed breaths. C bring hips & head towards each other on the left side with back at normal level. breathe in. D bring hips and head towards each other on right side, breathe out. alternate these two for several relaxed breaths. Then do a whole circle: A - C - B - D for several relaxed breaths. Then reverse direction.

the lion: cross one bent knee over the other and place both hands on knees arms straight. open your eyes as wide as you can. open your mouth as wide as you can. Stick out your tongue. hold several relaxed breaths. good for sore throats!

the camel: sit on your calves. Then rise up straight from your knees, place hands upon heels and lean back head. hold several relaxed breaths and return to kneeling or go into the fish position (next).

the fish: from a kneeling or camel pose bring palms together on chest and bring head back to the floor. hold several relaxed breaths. Use back to help yourself up to kneeling position.

head to knee stretch: sit with one leg straight out and the other bent so that the foot rests on the thigh (or sole against inside of thigh) palms together stretch spine up, then stretch head to knee and clasp foot (or ankle). hold several breaths. Then do other leg. then stretch to both knees.

the cobbler: sit with knees bent out and soles of feet together. bring feet as near to body and knees as near to floor as possible. Keep spine straight. hold several breaths. stretch head to feet. hold several breaths. return to sitting.

the tortoise: sit with knees slightly bent bring head, shoulders to floor between legs and thrust arms back under thighs. hold several relaxed breaths and sit up. 137

open stretch: Sit up straight with legs straight and feet as far apart as they'll go comfortably. stretch over to one ankle holding foot in both hands. Then up straight and do other side. Then hold one ankle (or foot) in each hand and bring head to floor. hold each position several relaxed breaths.

the lotus and the half-lotus: sit with spine straight and belly in with legs crossed indian style. Place one foot on the thigh of the other leg. (half lotus). Place other foot on thigh of first leg. (lotus). hold whichever is comfortable for as many relaxed breaths as you can.

yoga mudra: the symbol of union. Sit in lotus. join hands behind back with arms straight. bring head to floor. hold several breaths. also you can do a shoulder stand in the lotus position.

rest: at the end of asanas rest on your back with your palms up next to your thighs for many relaxed breaths.

spinal twist: sit with right knee bended under left thigh and left foot outside of right thigh. hold left foot in right hand with arm straight & elbow on left side of right knee. bend left arm around back with hand on waistline as far around as you can. hold several breaths. do it on the other side.

another lion: from lotus come forward so you rest on your hands and knees. Open eyes and mouth as wide as you can. stick your tongue out. hold several relaxed breaths.

head stand: make a triangle of your forearms and the space between your elbows (all sides equal.) rest your head between your clasped hands. with your legs straight, "walk" up to your head until your back raises you up and your legs straighten. hold several relaxed breaths and come down the way you came up.

environment

139

away from civilization one need only quiet one's mind
to be in paradise. when you move there, though, be
sensitive to local social codes, so that your public
appearance makes you blend in harmoniously. no
need to blow your neighbors' minds, even if
cosmic experiences move you to change your own life.
140 and leave no tracks. leave your campsites as
if no one had ever been there. respect people's privacy.

the ideal human climate is one where clothes, shoes, houses, heating, cooking are not necessary. our species lived that way before the first civilization. if you can raise what you like to eat, you're probably in your own ideal climate. all you need is sense enough to go outdoors when the sun is shining.

141

there is no doubt that a tree makes the best house.
the most tranquil room combines natural and handmade useful
and beautiful objects, green growing plants & emptiness in a light and
airy space constructed of natural materials, such as wood, stone,
thatch, bamboo and adobe. Ideally each bed should be in its own
structure, out of eyesight & earshot of other structures. a round house,
a tipi or a dome makes an indoor space more like the universe
and less like a box. floor level sitting encourages a stronger back.
no electricity puts you on a healthy solar rhythm. living areas are
142 defined by your day: sleeping & meditation (when it's inclement weather), preparation
of food, bathing & laundry, playing music & arts & crafts, dining & sitting around.

we like to hang cut-out
paper stars from the
ceiling because walking
through them is like
walking through the heavens,
and because breezes turn them so they
disappear (when they're sideways to you)
& twinkle, and paper moons go through
phases. colored cut-out rainbow lady
smiles blessings 'round the room. use
stiff paper. take needle & thread to make
a hole at the top & tie thread through it.
tie other end to tape, tack or through a canopy.

143

to start a woodfire: hold a magnifying glass over some crumpled paper, straw & thin kindling wood. the sun's rays, concentrated by the glass, will eventually cause the kindling to smolder. Fan it gently, and when it is flaming, gradually add bigger pieces of wood.

using solar energy at home...

parabolic mirrors: (above) the sunlight is focussed into the center and to a point above the center, where a cooking pot, water heater or oven may be placed. a solar furnace for high temperature metal work utilizes many parabolic mirrors all focussed on the kiln. easy water heater: coil 200 feet of ¾ inch black plastic hose running from water source to bathing place, either across a sunny meadow or on the roof.

communities fall generally into two lifestyles:
those with one kitchen for everybody and
those in which each house has its own.
communities come in so many varieties
that people can pick the most harmonious
with their individual lifestyles.
the purpose of the intentional commune
is to provide as much leisure as possible
for all its members. some leisure-preserving
precautions for communal groups:

   don't freak out the locals.
   don't encourage visitors.
   don't exceed the number of residents your
      land can support.
   pay attention to the land & weather: feed
      the soil, pick up the garbage, keep cars
      & polluting chemicals off it.
   no leaders. instead, a tribe of volunteers.

communal living is the best for children, because there are many kids and adults to relate to. parents can take turns watching them, leaving others free to be other places. communes focused on their own schools are the best.

GOD BLESS OUR FREE STORE

RAGS & SCRAP CLOTH

KITCHEN WARE

TOOLS & METAL PARTS

SOCKS

PANTS

TOYS

SHIRTS

. . . . . possessions . . . .

as needs are simplified & communal trust
blossoms, ownership gives way to usership;
unused things are put in the community's
free store to be recycled into another house-
hold. In a magical way, everyone finds
what he needs, & money becomes less & less necessary.
when moving out of a house, each person leaves
what he can for the next person & travels
light. artists create beautiful things just
to watch them circulate in the flow of usership.

147

relationships

living on land held in common brings deep
relationships with others living there, often
lasting for lifetimes. Sometimes it is
hard to find time to be alone, because everyone
who drops by is one of your closest friends.
a sign on the door or a verbal request
sometimes fills the function of a telephone.
when several dwellings are on the same
canyon, it acts as an amplifier & echo
chamber for long distance communications.

148

canyon calls

each person has his own identifying call:
a yodel, a hoot, a cheer, a whistle, a laugh,
a song, a howl, a moo, any animal's call
or any kind of funny sound. distantly
approaching an encampment, a visitor
lets out his personal canyon call to announce
who is coming and the replying call will
tell who is there to welcome him. Silence
tells that no one is there or that no visitors
are wanted. a canyon call can also be a
mantra (a word or words inducing god-consciousness).

Sunday feasts are
pot luck dinners
with everyone both listening & performing happy music
together & dancing. a sauna bath or swimming
or watching a lunar eclipse or celebrating birthdays
& weddings & visiting gurus go well with Sunday
feasts. each one is different, but all are wonderful
because all are hosts and all are guests.

work day parties

are gatherings to do a project; preparing the soil
for a garden, raising a roof, collecting & recycling
garbage, building a dam are more fun with
music & lemonade. morning & evening milking
sometimes draws singers & bakers of hot biscuits.

151

meetings for discussing community business can be run with best results when only one person talks at a time. A stone or a shell can be passed around the meeting circle; whoever holds it may speak; if they have nothing to say they pass it on. In a community of leaderless volunteers, every voice carries equal weight.

sometimes groups of people get so high & so close
in their interrelating that they feel at one with
each other and with the universe. some
of our group religious experiences
came out of these events:

a feast in which everyone
fed everyone except themselves
(with their hands)

sleeping in a circle with all
the feet in the center, alternating
men & women.

witnessing together a birth,
marriage, wake, eclipse,
sunset, sunrise, meteor.
working together at thankless tasks.

chanting AUM while
hugging in a circle.

singing & dancing &
playing music together
with abandon.

taking a sacrament.

neighborhood silence fast.

living on open land.

OH FRIENDS

a minor   G   F   E⁷

oh friends tell me why there's but one per-son brea-thing oh
friends tell me why there's but one mind sha-ring oh
source of all life --- all bliss -- be-sto-wing oh

a minor   G   F   G⁷

friends tell me why there's but one heart bea-ting oh
friends tell me why there's but one bo-dy ca-ring oh
bro-thers and sis-ters with ra--diance glo-wing u-

C   C   C⁷   F

friends tell me why there's but one soul be-ing is it
friends tell me why must I die in the da-ring is it
-nite now with all o'er the whole earth flo-wing it is

C   G⁷   C   E⁷

life is it light is it love ---- oh
life is it light is it love ----- oh
life it is light it is love.

RS '67
153

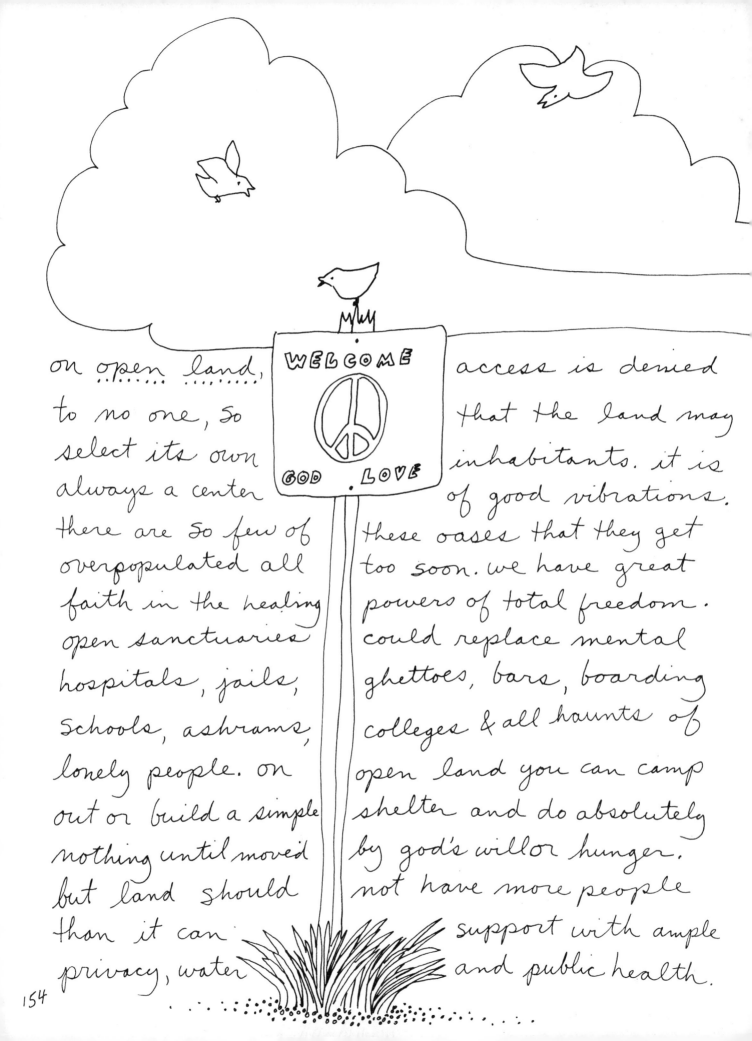

on open land,
to no one, so
select its own
always a center
there are so few of
overpopulated all
faith in the healing
open sanctuaries
hospitals, jails,
schools, ashrams,
lonely people. on
out or build a simple
nothing until moved
but land should
than it can
privacy, water

access is denied
that the land may
inhabitants. it is
of good vibrations.
these oases that they get
too soon. we have great
powers of total freedom.
could replace mental
ghettoes, bars, boarding
colleges & all haunts of
open land you can camp
shelter and do absolutely
by god's will or hunger.
not have more people
support with ample
and public health.

Solitude is peace & quiet and freedom to do as you please. Alone in nature you find her rhythms as your living pattern, an enlightening balm for the nerves.

Solitude is only depressing if done indoors all the time. days spent silently observing & listening to nature are full of unexpected delights.

health

talk to your body.
tell your body to be well.
appreciate its services.
stroke the tender parts.
encourage strength & grace
& relaxation.

talk to plants
tell them to grow green.
love them; touch them.
encourage beauty.

talk to nature
tell the universe
to be peaceful.
thank all things
for being.
serve anything
or anyone
in need.
encourage
all beings
to bliss.

everything has consciousness & can respond.

157

good food makes good health

each person's needs are different. organically
grown or wild foods which you gathered
yourself from where you live are the most
harmonious with your individual system,
especially if you chew them well. not eating
when not hungry is good for you. make
all dietary changes gradually. food is made
158 of sunlight & earth & should be gathered with love.

as the cells of your body absorb each substance
you eat, they send messages of well-being or
illness to your perceptive centers. to find your
own perfect   diet, eat very slowly

eating as a meditation

& chew each mouthful as many times as you
can. feel the effects of each food on your stomach,
intestines, and throughout your body. Our findings
so far: well-being foods . . . . illness foods

well-being foods

kale, collards, chard, spinach,
mustard greens, broccoli leaves (raw)
raw garlic, wheat grass juice, carrot juice,
papaya (with seeds), pineapple juice with brewer's
yeast, raw goat milk yogurt, mangoes, oranges,
passionfruit, pineapple, apples, berries, alfalfa
sprouts, tofu (soy bean curd), avocado, kelp,
herbal tea: alfalfa, mint, camomile, papaya leaf, rose
hips, wheat germ oil, chia seeds, watercress, parsley

illness foods

white sugar, white flour, anything
containing insecticides, artificial
sweeteners, hormone injections,
preservatives; boiled vegetables,
prepared supermarket foods,
fermented tea, lard, margarine,
(all solidified fats), instant
foods, artificial or processed
dairy foods, monosodium glutamate.

illness is purification

sickness is the body's way of eliminating toxic
substances when it is overcome with them.
vomiting, diarrhea, fever & sweat, pus-filled abcesses are
all emergency cleansing measures. Industrially
produced food, polluted air & water are the sources
of the toxins. When the body is free of these toxins
it never is sick. One can eliminate toxins
through pure diet & fasting, but unless these changes
are made gradually & with attention to the
nutritional needs of the body, the elimination
may be so rapid that it becomes sickness.
rest up, keep warm, & drink lots of liquids.

160

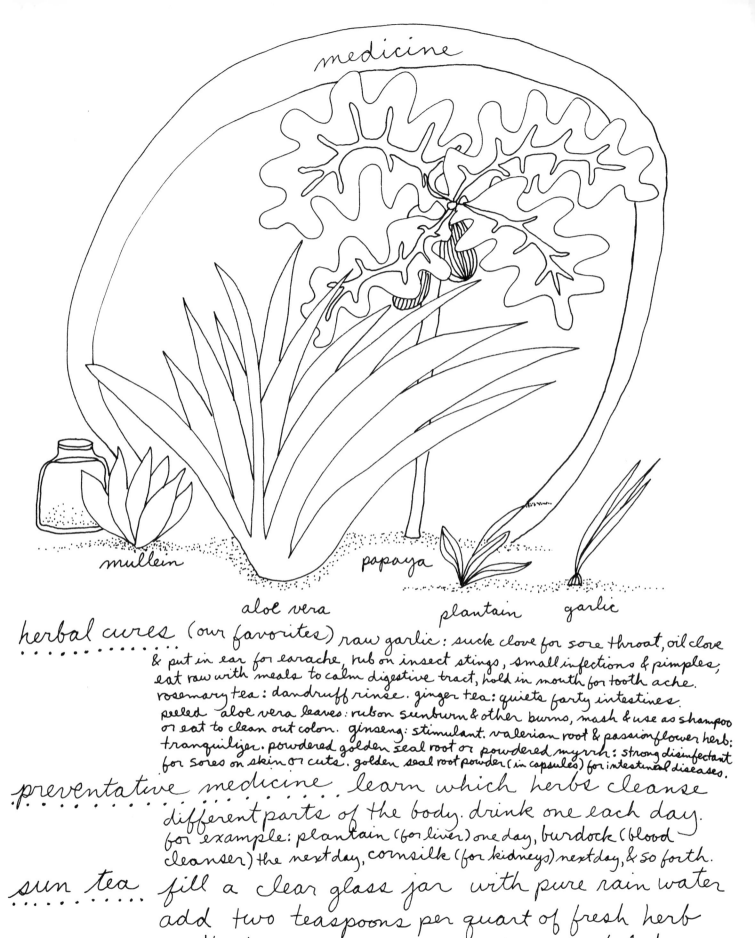

medicine

mullein

aloe vera

papaya

plantain

garlic

herbal cures (our favorites) raw garlic: suck clove for sore throat, oil clove
& put in ear for earache, rub on insect stings, small infections & pimples;
eat raw with meals to calm digestive tract, hold in mouth for tooth ache.
rosemary tea: dandruff rinse. ginger tea: quiets farty intestines.
peeled aloe vera leaves: rub on sunburn & other burns, mash & use as shampoo
or eat to clean out colon. ginseng: stimulant. valerian root & passionflower herb:
tranquilizer. powdered golden seal root or powdered myrrh: strong disinfectant
for sores on skin or cuts. golden seal root powder (in capsules) for intestinal diseases.

preventative medicine learn which herbs cleanse
different parts of the body. drink one each day.
for example: plantain (for liver) one day, burdock (blood
cleanser) the next day, cornsilk (for kidneys) next day, & so forth.

sun tea fill a clear glass jar with pure rain water
add two teaspoons per quart of fresh herb
or 1½ teaspoons per quart of dry herb. let
stand in sunlight, shake well three times
per day, for three days. strain & serve.

body meditations

sensing systems: close eyes. observe breathing. feel which muscles are tense. concentrate on your lungs, stomach, liver, all organs one at a time. you may even be able to feel your nervous system when you totally relax.

fart cure: (above) clasp knees to chest. inhale. hold slowly release. repeat until farts are gone.

hiccup cure: breathe deeply. hold your inhale. slowly exhale. hold empty. slowly inhale. hold again: repeat three times.

inside information: look at your shit. whatever was undigested should be eliminated from your diet in the future. a perfect diet means a perfect shit—it doesn't require toilet paper.

162

shitting into a hole in the earth is good
for you & for the trees. it should be buried
at least one foot deep & never uphill from or
near a water supply. a post hole digger
(above) makes a small round deep hole in
minutes. Squatting tones the leg, back &
abdominal muscles. if you must use a flush
toilet, squatting instead of sitting protects you
from hemorrhoids & constipation. a swedish
anaerobic unit converts shit & organic garbage
into sterile odorless compost; flush toilets
pollute waterways. while meditating on sunlight,
you can fulfill your deepest earthy role as
builder of the soil and gardener of galaxies. 163

all places where water springs
from the earth are holy. hot springs
especially are medicine for people.
Some sulphur springs contain traces of
arsenic, which in such small doses is
hallucinogenic. But sitting in water hotter
than your body temperature is naturally
tranquilizing anyway. (don't scald your skin
steam clouds make good meditation points
If you can alternate the hot baths with dip
in an icy cold stream your skin
& circulation get to pulsating. the
sulphur is good for curing infections
in the skin. be sure to oil your skin
well after rinsing
off the sulphur
water. please don't
pollute the springs
with
soap...

keeping silence
is a good way to stop
thinking and automatically saying things
and initiating useless discussions.
silence absorbs thoughts and cures
attention addictions. Instead, the sounds
of nature permeate you and soon
you hear the AUM of the universe
that was always droning
behind everything but was
drowned out by thoughts. listen
to your breathing, your
pulse, the wind & rivers.

165

passion, joy, grief & anger really are emotional explosions. But there is a difference between self-expression and freaking out just to manipulate other people. consider the consequences for others, even for yourself before getting all wrought up about anything. usually it's not worth it. in solitude & silence & sunshine one may find one's cares begi to evaporate as trembling breaths slow down & tight assholes relax. try humming through you lips while sticking out your tongue.

worry
. . . .
animals get their daily worrying done by chewing
bones, grass, seaweed, hides, bark or leaves.
people chew with their heads, gnawing old
problems & imagining future ones. bring worry
back to the body level by sucking your thumb
or a pacifier or
licorice root or
some tough
sundried
apricots. or
chomp on
carrots,
celery or
cabbage.
common
worrybone
substitutes:
chewing gum,
smoking,
compulsive
talking
or
eating.

167

often an unrelaxed state is due to
nutritional deficiencies.. Niacinamide
(a B vitamin found in brewer's yeast), calcium
(in milk) and vitamin A (carrot juice or a
salad of raw spinach, collards, chard &
mustard greens) are all essential to the
nervous system. Also a noisy, electrical
environment or lack
of solitude may be
the root of tension.
In any case, the
less you believe
bad things will
happen and the more
you believe good
things will happen,
the more it works
out that way. It's
just a question
of raising your
bliss toleration
level.

if you're in sore need of
relaxation, take a long hot
bath, drink some valerian
root & passion flower herb tea,
and lie on a bed or a
hammock, expand-   ing your asshole
when you inhale   and contracting
it when you exhale,   and if possible
have someone you   love massage
you with oil.

sitting around all day long brings great rewards
in relaxation. No day spent sitting around
170 is wasted unless it is done nervously.

if you are full of energy
and don't want to sit around
you can quiet your mind
by performing mindless
activity such as hiking
in wilderness, hatha yoga,
swimming, surfing,
dancing, gardening, cutting
firewood, gathering food,
singing, playing a
musical instrument,
potting, weaving,
sweeping, dusting,
washing things,
painting things,
or taking a
bath.

sunbathing

we like to lie
in the semi-shade
to spare our skin
the wear & tear of overexposure.
peoples who have lived for centuries
near the equator have lots
of oil & pigment in

their skin, but we must oil ours before & after
sunbathing to keep it moist. nude sunbaths
are safe only after previously unexposed parts
have gradually become pigmented. your skin
has to last a lifetime – no use wearing it out
with overdoses of direct sunlight. blemished
skin, sore throats & yeasty genitals heal faster
with exposure to sunlight. to reduce muscular
aches, sit in sunlight wrapped in a dark blanket
or inside a closed sunny window.

living naked

after one day of living outdoors naked your skin feels radiant and tingling. fresh air circulates on your skin instead of little pockets of stale air caught under layers of cloth. you become aware of your muscles, bones, skin, glands, organs as you never were when covered with clothes. after several days the temperature variation you are comfortable in will widen. the sunlight absorbed by your skin will give you both serenity and a decrease in appetite. but observe sunbathing precautions and avoid being in public view.

173

loose fitting clothes allow air to flow on the skin. choose the most flowing & serene fabrics to surround your body. Use draw strings.
shoes the major nerves of the body terminate in the feet. Rigid bulky soles & elevated heels set the body off balance. Toes need air & room to spread out. on pavement wear rubber-soled shoes to absorb the shock. soft light-weight shoes allow the body to move with grace.

174

tightly bound hair creates tension in the
body. jewelry puts extra weights & stress that
inhibit free movement. Cosmetics pollute the skin
& soaps dry it. Oils aid healing & elasticity. a
massage of wheat germ oil after each bath makes
the skin deliciously soft and smooth.

175

taking a sacrament

a sacrament is a soul medicine whi
opens your awareness of the here & nou
to the point where you may experience
the void, the deity, or have visions. they
have made available to anyone these
experiences without years of discipline
and thus are a good cure for spiritual
pride (holier-than-thou-ness). however
most of them are presently illegal.
if you take them, be far from civilizatio
in a gentle natural environment and
only with people you love who are serene
if someone is having a difficult
experience with a sacrament, encourag
the person to lie down on a comfortable
bed and suck his thumb. give him some
niacinamide tablets or brewer's yeast
blended in pineapple juice.

being of the sunday.
one day a week (any day) put aside all survival
activities and sit in nature observing the sunlight.
prepare food the day before so nothing need be done
by you or anyone else. by being of the sun one
day a week you can live on the earth without
getting caught up in the follies of civilization.
on being of the sunday
it's a good day to do some
of the things in this book.

when you have perfected your health, and your aura shows you to be without malice towards any being, and when you have totally relaxed & deconditioned to your god nature, and you know the healing powers of sunlight, herbs, good diet, silence, solitude, and all the preventative medicines, you are a sun healer. if you help others it will be without reward or payment and with the total consent of the recipient. although you may not practice medicine without a license, you may nurse the sick & unhappy after they have satisfied their need for professional help.

the more radiant sun healers & happy yogis
of all kinds walk upon the earth, the closer
we come to the golden age, when all beings
exist in perfect harmony once again.

INDEX (also may be read as a poem)

183

hope you found
what you're
looking for.

books on related subjects

· ·

visions "warriors of the rainbow" by william willoya &
· · · · · · · · · ·
vinson brown, naturegraph press, 1962

"burnt toast" by peter gould, alfred a. knopf 1971

"the teachings of don juan: a yaqui way of knowledge"
by carlos castaneda, ballantine books 1968

"a separate reality" & "journey to ixtlan" both by
carlos castaneda, simon & schuster 1971 & 1972

"in the kingdom of mescal" by georg schafer &
nan cuz, shambala books (berkeley) 1970

"black elk speaks" by john neihardt,
university of nebraska press, 1961

light body "satprem, sri aurobindo, or adventures in
· · · · · · · · · ·
consciousness" sri aurobindo society,
sri aurobindo ashram, pondicherry, india
second edition, 1970

the wheel of the ages "the holy science" by swami sri
· · · · · · · · · · · · · ·
yukteswar. self realization fellowship,
los angeles, 1972

the fall away: "Typee" (novel) by Herman Melville
& "children of the rainbow" by leinani Melville
theosophical publishing house, wheaton illinois
1969

the dawning of light: "Test Pattern for living"
by nicholas johnson, avon books 1972

"Providencia" (poems in spanish) by gonzalo arango
plaza & janes, barcelona, spain, 1972

the elemental yogas: earth: "living the good life" & "the maple sugar book" by helen & scott nearing, both from schocken books, new york 1970, 1971

"living on the earth" by alicia bay laurel, vintage books 1971

water: "sense awareness below your mind" by bernard gunther, collier books, 1968

air: "whole earth catalogue" portola institute or random house

fire: "yoga sutras of patanjali" translated by C. Johnstone, weiser, new york.

"the zen teachings of huang-po: on the transmission of mind" translated by john blofeld, grove press, new york 1959

"the way of life" (the book of tao by lao-tse) translated by bynner witter, capricorn press (santa barbara), 1944.

"be here now" by baba ram dass, lama foundation 1971 (available from crown publishers)

"monday night class" & "the caravan" by stephen gaskin, book farm (berkeley) 1970 and random house 1972.

primate consciousness "my friends, the wild chimpanzees" by jane lawick-goodall, national geographic.

"the naked ape" by desmond morris, dell 1967

"kinship with all life" by j. allen boone, harper & row 1954

193

sun lore graphis magazine, march 1962, 100th issue "THE
SUN IN ART" from amstutz & herdeg, graphis press,
zurich, switzerland.

clouds & weather "instant weather forecasting" by
alan watts, dodd & mead, new york 1968

care of trees "the 1949 U.S. yearbook of agriculture-tree
published by Superintendent of Documents,
Washington, D.C.
pamphlets on care of trees, order from
agricultural extension service,
University Hall, University of California
at Berkeley, Berkeley, California 94720

hypnotic states (how to induce them, with suggestion
which can be listened to during trance:)
"Passages" by louis savary & marianne
andersen, harper & row, 1972

the solar system as a vibrating string. "theory of
celestial influence" by rodney collins,
weiser publications.

modes, scales, tunings, homemade musical instruments
"genesis of a music" by harry partch, new
edition in process from da capo press, new york.
"the greek aulos" by kathleen schlesinger,
metheun & co., london, 1939 (out of print).(on grass flute
"northern indian music" by alain danielou,
praeger, new york, 1969

194

nodes, etc. continued "an introduction to the study
of musical scales" by alain danielou,
the india society, london, 1943 (out of print).

sundials popular mechanics, july 1970, pages 134-175
scientific american august 1967, pages 137-139

songs & ceremonies "cosmic chants" by paramahansa
yogananda, self-realization fellowship
los angeles, california 1963
"the earth mass" by joe pintauro (with
pictures by alicia bay laurel), harper & row, 1972
"the sacred pipe: black elk's account of
the seven rites of the oglala sioux" edited
by joseph e. brown, university of oklahoma
press, 1953 (also available from penguin books)

massage "the art of sensual massage" by gordon
inkeles & murray todris, straight arrow
books, new york, 1971

breathing "the seven yogas of naropa" essay in
"esoteric teachings of the tibetan tantra"
edited by muses-chang, falcon wing press,
switzerland, 1963

mandala "mandala" by jose & miriam arguelles,
shambala books, berkeley, 1972

mudra "mudra: a study of symbolic gestures in
japanese buddhist sculpture" by e. dale
saunders, princeton university press.

hatha yoga "integral hatha yoga book" by swami
satchitananda, H, R & Winston, new york, 1970

hatha yoga, continued. "light on yoga" by B.K.S. Iyengar, allen & unwin, ltd., london, 1965

solar power "wind & solar energy: proceedings of the new delhi symposium" UNESCO publication 1956, 19 avenue kleber, paris-16ᵉ, france. "proceedings of the united nations conference on new sources of energy" volume 1-introducti volume 2 & 3 geothermal energy, volume 4,5,6, solar energy, volume 7 wind energy. available from sales section, united nations, new york 10017

children "nature's children: a guide to organic foods & herbal remedies for children" by juliette de bairacli-levy, schocken books, new york 1971 "summerhill" by a.s. neill, hart publishing co., 1960 (about free schools) "the rasberry exercises" by salli rasberry & robert greenway, distributed by book people, berkeley, calif. 1970 (about free schools) 3 coloring books by alicia bay laurel: "happy day, cried the rainbow lady, full of light" "sylvie sunflower" and "the family of families" from harper & row, 1972

communes "alternatives journal" box 36604, los angeles, 90036 (also by editor richard fairfield by photographer consuelo sandoval, several books: "communes in europe", "communes in japan", "communes USA")

open land request newsletter & manifesto from ahimsa church, box 81, bodega bay, california, 94923 (wheeler & morningstar ranch).

solitude in nature. "walden" by henry david thoreau, doubleday, new york.

diet. "let's eat right to keep fit" by adelle davis, harcourt brace & world, new york
"the natural foods cookbook" by beatrice trum hunter, pyramid books, 1967
"back to eden" by jethro kloss, longview publishing house 1939
"vermont folk medicine" by d.c. jarvis, m.d. faucett crest books 1958
"vital foods for total health" by bernard jenson
"diet for a small planet" by frances lappe moore, ballantine books, new york, 1971
"the mucus-less diet", "rational fasting" (& several other books) by arnold ehret.

hot springs. "thermal springs of the western united states" (37 page reprint from out-of-print "thermal springs of the United States & other countries of the world, a summary" by gerald waring, which could once be gotten from the Superintendent of Documents, U.S. government printing office, washington, D.C., for $2.75) but now can be ordered from:
paradise publishers
box 5372
santa barbara, california 93103

sun calendar. can be ordered from Katharsis, 228 delano street, san francisco, california, 94112. (hope they do one for next year!)

appendix B: materials: where to find them

parts for sunstrobes, solar cells, etc:

      pacific radio
      1300 cahuenga blvd.
      los angeles, calif. 90028

parts for light shows, prisms, reflective surface,
      telescopes, weather balloons, & so forth:

      edmund scientific co.
      300 edscorp building
      barrington, new jersey 08007
      (request free catalogue)

piano string in bulk, tuning hammers, wire for most
      stringed instruments:

      tuner's supply co.
      1274 folsom st.
      san francisco, calif. 94103

dulcimer, guitar, harp (kits & already made

   V. E. Hughes   lyn elder
   8665 W. 13th ave   magic mountain
   Denver, Colorado 80215   workshop
                      box 614
                      mill valley, calif. 9494

papaya-based raw food nutrition bars (to supplement
     raw fruit & vegetable diet & cleanse body)
      papaya hill
      box A
      paia, hawaii 96779

healthful rope-soled shoes with woven cotton tops in white or colored stripes. send tracing of your foot and international money order for $2 to:

> R. Jones
> apartado aereo 888
> Popayán, Colombia

(specify white or striped tops)

toilet unit digests shit & raw organic kitchen wastes into odorless, sterile compost in 6 months to one year:

> Clivus composter
> A. B. Clivus
> Tonstigen 6
> S-13500
> Tyresö
> sweden

herbs, perfumed oils (request free catalogue)
> nature's herb company
> 281 ellis street
> san francisco, calif. 94102

nassage oils & perfumed oils:
> the body shop
> shattuck at berkeley way
> berkeley, calif.

appendix C: anatomy of the human eye

the human eye consists of a lens & a shutter that opens & shuts according to the amount of light shining on it — (the less the amount of light, the more it opens) and a screen of rods & cones on which the light is projected at the back of the eye. If these rods & cones are subjected to intense light, such as the direct rays of the sun, they can become permanently damaged; that is, you can be blinded. for this reason we urge our readers not to look directly at the sun or at brilliant reflections of the sun. If your eyes feel the slightest irritation when you are in the sunshine, close your eyes or go into the shade.

be conscious of all parts of your body and you'll enjoy them more.

acknowledgments · · · · · · · · · · · · · ·

everyone we ever met or heard of made some contribution to this work, but since it was written in the sunshine, a great deal of credit goes to the sun. we would also like to thank graphis magazine – for permission to quote from their anniversary issue "THE SUN IN ART" (march 1962) pp. 23 & 31) and also grove press for permission to quote from the Zen teachings of huang-po. (p. 120) (both of these publications are listed in the bibliography). a special thanks goes to brian vermeersch, andrea lenox, jaya bransten, & alice rosengard for researching publisher's names & stuff for the bibliography & also illuminating some obscurities in the text. thank you, tron hickman, for showing us the sunstrobe. Thanks are due also to our editor, frances mc cullough, & our agent, mary clemmey, for taking on our project. But most of all, a special loving hug to sol ray, who waited while we wrote this book. we love you!

this is not the end

because our learning of sun yoga will continue
as days of sunshine go by
and everyone & everything teaches us more.
thank you for visiting our book
hope you're having a good time
now and forever! ♡ Ramón & Alicia

202